Once Upon A Soul

Once Upon A Soul

Stories of Striving and Yearning

by

Hanoch Teller

New York City Publishing Company

© Copyright 1984 by Hanoch Teller, 46/7 Arzei Habira, Jerusalem 97761, Israel.
All Rights Reserved. No individual or institution may reproduce this work in whole or in part **in any form,** without written permission from the copyright holder, except by a reviewer who wishes to quote brief selections for magazine or newspaper reviews.

THE RIGHTS OF THE COPYRIGHT HOLDERS WILL BE STRICTLY ENFORCED.

ISBN 0—9614772-3-7

Library of Congress Registration No. TX 2-313-060

SECOND EDITION

12   11   10   9

Distributed by:
FELDHEIM PUBLISHERS
200 Airport Executive Park
Spring Valley, NY 10977

J. Lehmann
Hebrew Booksellers
20 Cambridge Terrace
Gateshead
Tyne & Wear

*To the memory of the millions
whose stories are now known
only to God.*

לעילוי נשמת
האשה החשובה מרת רבקה שפירא ע"ה
בת הרב ר' משה אליעזר זצ"ל אב"ד דאטלנטיק סיטי, ארה"ב
נכדת הגה"צ ר' בן ציון ב"ר ר' הירש מיכל זצוק"ל

שהקדישה מכוחותיה לבריות במסירות ובסבר פנים יפות

ת.נ.צ.ב.ה.

ALSO BY HANOCH TELLER

Soul Survivors
'Souled'
The Steipler Gaon
Sunset
Courtrooms of the Mind
Above the Bottom Line
Bridges of Steel, Ladders of Gold

APPROBATION FROM HAGAON HARAV MOSHE FEINSTEIN ZT"L

RABBI MOSES FEINSTEIN
455 F. D. R. DRIVE
New York, N. Y. 10002

ORegon 7-1222

משה פיינשטיין
ר"מ תפארת ירושלים
בנוא יארק

ב"ה

ב' ניסן תשמ"ה

לכבוד מוהר"ר העניך טעללער שליט"א, בברכת שלום וברכה וכט"ס.

Due to the delicate state of my health, it is difficult for me to delve into books sent to me for endorsement. However, I heard wonderful tidings regarding your most recent as well as your earlier book, from my grandson HaRav Mordechai Tendler, Shlita. He praised the books as ones which can provide a great service in drawing the hearts of many of our brethren to their Father in Heaven. Therefore, I offer my blessings that the Almighty will award you with much success with this book, and that you may merit to increase and glorify the Torah I have instructed that my seal be impressed upon this letter.

Moshe Feinstein

אחדשה"ט
הנה פחמת
להסכמה,
מוהר"ר פ
של הרבה
השי"ח בם
וצוחי שישימו חרחמתי על מכחב זה.

APPROBATION FROM HAGAON HARAV SHLOMO ZALMAN AUERBACH SHLITA

הרב שלמה זלמן אויערבאך
פעיה"ק ירושלים תובב"א

ב"ה, יום...

I hereby express my most heartfelt blessing to my dear friend, Rabbi Hanoch Yonason Teller, who studies in the Kollel of the Mirrer Yeshiva. I know him very well and can veritably testify that he is a fearer of sin and a Torah scholar.

Since he is in the category of a *talmid chacham* who does not allow anything improper to emanate from his hands, not to mention knows how to word things pleasantly and correctly, his intention to publish a book of his stories about Torah leaders and loving ones fellow Jew, etc.; in order to strengthen faith in God and enhance mitzva observance for an English reading audience receives my thorough endorsement. I extol his actions and extend my blessings that his words will penetrate the hearts of his readers and influence them to uplift and improve their deeds and purify their outlook for their own everlasting benefit.

May the author be blessed for his efforts from the source of blessing as he so desires, and I so fervently wish.

Shlomo Zalman Auerbach

Contents

Approbations	**VIII**
Preface	**XI**
Introduction	**XIII**
❦ **A Time for Everything Under the Heaven**	**17**
Encounters in flight	
The Charitable Charter	19
Up Up and Avey	27
❦ **A Time to Embrace**	**33**
Collection of Biographies	
Reb Hirsh Michal's Yerushalayim shel Ma'alah	35
(Rabbi Yehoshua Zvi Michel Shapiro)	
Remembering the Chofetz Chaim	50
(Rabbi Yisrael Meir Kagan)	
The Vision of Yechezkel	59
(Rabbi Yechezkel Abramsky)	
The Last Hundred Days	76
(Rabbi Chaim Leib Shmulevitz)	
A Purim Passing	83
(Rabbi Yosef Binyomin Rubin)	
❦ **A Time to Mend**	**89**
Soviet Jews Rediscover their Judaism	
Lail Shimurim	91
Raising His Voice	96

❦ A Time to Keep — 101
The Performance of Mitzvos

The Day of the Donkey	103
A Kesuba for our Anniversary	107
Mighty Men of Valor	112
Something New Under the Sun	118
Hospitality is Homemade	122
When There's Hope There's Life	126

❦ A Time to Rend — 133
Reflections on Destruction

Where Are the Scars	135
Rosita's Legacy	142

❦ A Time to Gather Stones — 147
Moments in Israel

My Jerusalem	149
Bible Anyone?	153
Ohr Somayach Furlough	164
Marking the Conclusion of a Beginning	171
The Cedars of Lebanon	176
The Explosion Which Shook up Bayit Vegan	183

❦ A Time to Heal — 187
A Chanukah Perspective

...Into the Hands of the Pure	189

❦ Glossary — 211

ב"ה

PREFACE

This book is the one-pound end product of a process. Its raw materials included eighty-four pounds of paper, sixteen typewriter ribbons, dozens of quills; as well as thoughts, emotions and research which cannot be quantified.

The process itself is rather unique. Unlike the sculptor, the story-writer has no clay to mold. Unlike the carver, he does not begin with a block of wood. He is more like the weaver, supplied only with colored threads, from which he will simultaneously manufacture and decorate his textile. Armed with scenes witnessed and tales heard, I have attempted to weave for each a tapestry of inspiration.

If there is a single theme that unites the stories of this collection, all of which are true, I hope it is that. The biography of a *gadol*, the martyrdom of Chana and her seven sons, or simply the first-time performance of a mitzva — they all have the power to inspire if the reader will only allow the message to enter his heart.

I view this work as a group effort. It is difficult to differentiate between those who have helped me specifically with this book and those who have helped me over the years. My indebtedness extends to them all. A *gadol* who is no longer living, a *tzaddik* in Jerusalem, a *gemorah rebbe* in New York, the Mirrer *Rosh Yeshiva* in whose *kollel* I learn, naturally my parents... the list goes on and on. Influences from all can be discerned in these pages.

I thank, in particular, the *Jewish Woman's Outlook* and the *Jewish Observer* (whose esteemed editor, Rabbi Nisson Wolpin, has been exceptionally kind) for permitting me to reprint stories which have appeared in their pages. I am indebted to Rabbi Aaron Surasky, whose biography of Rabbi Yechezkel Abramsky in Hebrew helped me with my rendition. Special gratitude must also be expressed to the friends and neighbors who gave of their time and talent whenever asked, and to my expert and generous typist. As for my wife, I can only paraphrase the words of Rabbi Akiva: all that's mine is hers.

Among the many discarded titles for this book was one, "With the Help of God." It remains, nonetheless, the most accurate expression of my feelings about this undertaking. My everlasting debt of gratitude to the Almighty cannot, I realize be discharged with a mere prefatory acknowledgement.

In almost every case, the stories in this collection were written because I was touched by an event, a person, a scene. In writing about it, I hoped to capture some of what had inspired me, and transmit it to others. If I have succeeded in some small measure, perhaps therein lies the beginning of a more meaningful expression of thanks.

ומי יתן שמילותי יחדרו ללבות הקוראים ויושפעו
מהם, ויתקדש שם שמים.

Hanoch Teller
Jerusalem ת"ו
Rosh Chodesh Adar Aleph 5744/February 1984

Introduction

How can one convey the idea that the only true wealth is Torah — that a poor man can be made rich by its study? King David takes a poetic, aphoristic approach: "Your Torah is worth more to me than thousands of gold and silver."

But the Talmud relates a story. Hillel was too poor to pay the admission fee to yeshiva. Undaunted, he climbed to the roof of the academy where, lying with his ear to the skylight, he could hear Shemayah and Avtalyon expound the words of the living God.

One Friday, during the wintry month of Teves, snow began to fall. Hillel, oblivious to the snowstorm, remained sprawled over the skylight and continued to absorb the words of the great masters. Early the next morning, Shemayah turned to Avtalyon: "My brother," he said, "by this time every day the yeshiva is filled with light, but today it is still dark." They looked up towards the skylight and saw the outline of a man completely covered in snow. They rushed up to the roof, brought Hillel down and revived him.

The story of Hillel serves not merely to inspire the poor to study Torah; it obligates them (*Hillel michayev es ha'aniyim*). Such is the power of the story. Laws, dissertations and lectures speak to the brain; a story speaks to the *soul*.

The Torah, a book of laws, begins with stories. There is no more effective way to portray the great ideals of character it will subsequently command. An exposition of the laws of receiving guests, for example, could never convey the same message as an account of *Avraham Avinu*'s gracious hospitality. A treatise on business ethics would not make the same impression as does the recounting of Yaakov's dealings with Laban. A story grabs, engages, compels.

The Hebrew word for story is *sipur*. The root of *sipur* is the same as that of *sapir*— sapphire. "And they saw the God of Israel and under His feet was like a paved work of sapphire clear as the very heavens." (*Shmos* 24:10). A story clarifies like a jewel.

The Haggada describes how Rabbi Eliezer, Rabbi Joshua, Rabbi Elazar ben Azaryah, Rabbi Akiva and Rabbi Tarfon retold the story of the Exodus from Egypt through the night until their students came to them and said: "Our teachers, it is time to recite the morning *Shema*." In fact, the rabbis were not speaking about or discussing the Exodus. They were *mesaprim*— telling it over, reliving the story so that it would shine with the clarity of a sapphire. Indeed, so blinding was the resultant sparkle that they lost track of time.

Kol hamarbe lesapeir beyezias Mitzraim harey zeh meshubach — " The more one tells the story of the going out of Egypt the more praiseworthy is he." It is only through the telling and retelling of the tale that one can fulfill the obligation of actually seeing oneself as a participant in the Exodus itself.

History recounts the facts of a specific time; stories reveal the truths of eternity. Greek stories became myths which were instrumental in shaping civilizations. Our sages always knew that an anecdote, tale or fable could evoke dimensions of depth and breadth which could not be grasped any other way.

Perhaps such an explanation could be suggested for the words of *Shemona Esrei*: על הצדיקים ועל החסידים ועל זקני עמך בית ישראל ועל פליטת סופריהם "May Your compassion, Lord our God, be aroused upon the pious, and upon the leaders of Your people, the House of Israel, and upon the remnant of their sages..."

Many glorious periods in Jewish history were ended abruptly by persecution and oppression. Particularly since the great Destruction of this century, we are bereft of far more than the presence of those who perished. The simple piety and selfless devotion to God of all past generations seems to be gone forever.

But if those pious greats have left our world, at least their stories remain; stories which provide us with a glimpse of earlier times. Their stories live on and inspire as an everlasting memorial. Do not read *sofreihem*— פליטת סופריהם "the remnant of their sages," but rather *sipureihem,* "their stories— which are the remnant."

The story is told of the Baal Shem Tov who would walk to a particular spot in the forest, utter a special formula and an angel would appear. In the generation after the Baal Shem, others went to the same spot in the forest and repeated the same formula, but no angel appeared. Their descendants went to the specified place in the forest but did not know the formula. And we, who do not even know where the forest is, much less the particular spot in the forest... what is left to us of the power and greatness of the Baal Shem Tov? We have a great deal. We have the story.

THE CHARITABLE CHARTER

The late sixties (following the Six-Day War) saw a surge in the number of American yeshiva students learning in Israel. Trips to the Holy Land were financed by fledgling budgets and cheaper routes were constantly sought.

GAZING ACROSS the lobby of the Commodore Hotel in New York City, Mr. Maggid was struck dumb. Saffron-robed Hare Krishnas, handbill-equipped Jews for Jesus, and a gaggle of hirsute hippies dressed in bleached-out jeans and tattered rummage-sale sloganed T-shirts were sprawled all over the lobby. Guitar cases were apparently the latest thing in luggage.

As soon as he could regain his composure, Mr. Maggid turned to his 19-year-old son, Moish, and said:

"So, these are the charter group members you're flying to Eretz Yisrael with? What am I gonna tell your mother?"

Moish had to admit that this was more motley a crew than even he had anticipated. It was August 1975, and he was on his way to a distinguished yeshiva in Jerusalem where he planned to finally settle down to serious learning — pending the outcome of his *farheir* — the *Rosh Yeshiva*'s (yeshiva dean) oral exam.

ICELANDIC AIRLINES' special charter group rates were the answer to a yeshiva *bochur*'s prayer: $188 one-way to Brussels and you didn't really have to be part of an official group to qualify. But you *did* have to meet and arrive with the other "group" members before flight-time, and that's why the Maggids were in the lobby of the Commodore.

The Greenwich Village travel agency where Moish discovered the group deal looked a little seedy and disreputable, but Moish was nothing if not enterprising. The itinerary was Icelandic to Brussels, then Lufthansa to Vienna with stopover, and finally El Al to Israel. The flight departed from New York Thursday afternoon and arrived in Brussels early Friday morning. At 9:30 a.m., he would catch the only day flight to Vienna where he would have most of Friday and Shabbos with Uncle Avraham and *Tante* Gittle. After Shabbos, Moish would continue to Israel.

IN THE MEANTIME the flight arrangements looked a lot better than the company. It was best not to make his father too nervous.

> *"Don't worry, Dad. I'm sure all the weirdos will get off in Brussels and I promise I won't have anything to do with them. I'll just keep to myself and learn – I even have my gemorah in my hand luggage, see?"*

" '*Don't worry,*' he says? What do you mean, 'Don't worry?' What is that, your theme song? 'Don't worry' is what you said when you sat in on that course this summer at City College, the one on Christianity and the New Testament. '*Da mah lehashiv,*' you said, 'You have to know what to answer them.' And the next thing I know you're arguing with that Jews for Jesus fella in the middle of Grand Central Station. 'Don't worry?' It's just *mazel* I didn't have to come down to the Police Station to bail you out of jail!"

"But, Dad! It wasn't my fault! I wasn't looking for trouble. I was simply pointing out to the JJ solicitor the fallacies of his beliefs and he ran out of arguments. Is it my fault he jumped up on the table and started screaming: 'This Jew is persecuting me because of my religious convictions'?"

"No, Moishie, it's not your fault. It's never your fault. You don't have to look for trouble, trouble finds you. But this," taking in the whole lobby with one sweeping gesture, "this is just asking for it!"

A STEWARDESS started making rounds, checking tickets and directing the passengers to the airport bus. Mr. Maggid embraced his son.

"You're lucky it's Rosh Chodesh Elul and it's too late to change plans. Remember, don't fool around in Brussels or you'll miss your connecting flight. And don't start up with any meshugenehs or misguided Jews. And call me from Uncle Avraham's. And write to your mother the minute you get to Eretz Yisrael. And think carefully before you answer the Rosh Yeshiva's questions. And..."

"Okay, Dad. I know: 'Stay out of trouble.' Don't worry!"

"Foor gezunt!" Mr. Maggid called after his son, as Moish hurried off to catch up with the other passengers, thinking to himself:

"If I tell Ma about this, she'll have conniptions! Moishie with a bunch of hippies! These guys are already flying!..."

THE AIRPORT lounge was already crowded when Moish and his "group" arrived. Now it was packed and the floor littered with hippies and their debris. Numbers kept changing on the Arrivals and Departures screen to which all eyes were directed. From the vantage point of Moish's seat, he could just make out the letters on the screen: *Icelandic Airlines Flight 042* — delayed.

Nisht gefairlach, Moish thought. He still had a few hours leeway. But he *had* to arrive in Brussels in time for the only connecting flight to Vienna, otherwise he'd be stuck in Brussels for Shabbos and he didn't know a soul there.

He decided not to think about it, and study for his test instead. He opened his *gemorah* and quickly became engrossed in the *shakla vetarya* (talmudic discussion). Hours had passed until sudden movement all around him alerted him — his flight was being announced. Moish hastily looked up at the huge clock on the wall of the lounge — how could so much time have passed? He realized that catching the Vienna flight was going to be tight... but not impossible.

M OISH CHOSE a seat on the aisle near the front of the plane, so that he could make a speedy departure when it landed — may his luggage have a safe journey catching up with him! The choice had provided an unexpected bonus: located behind the galley he could easily overhear the stewardesses' gossip. Not that he intended to eavesdrop, God forbid. But you never know, maybe the plane would develop engine trouble — *chas veshalom!* — and it wouldn't hurt to have a little extra time for *Tehillim* (Psalms).

His attention riveted on the galley, Moish failed to notice the gentleman seated on his right. As takeoff approached, however, the sound of rattling beads coming from that direction distracted him and he turned his head towards his neighbor. To his astonishment, the adjacent seat was occupied by a priest, — a living, breathing, black-frocked, white-collared priest. Moish quickly closed his gaping mouth.

A Time for Everything Under the Heaven / 23

"What's that book you've got there, young man?"
Moish managed to find his tongue in time to answer politely, *"It's a volume of the Talmud, sir."*
"Oh, yes, the Talmud. The tales of the Rabbis..."
"Hardly tales," responded Moish, ready to jump into the fray.

The priest told Moish that he was on his way to attend a missionary conference in Europe. "We espouse a religion of love," he commenced. "Do unto others as you would have others do unto you. We aren't negative, blah, blah..." He launched into a well-rehearsed speech on the subject of comparative religions, unaware of his seat-mate's preparedness for debate. Moish had been through this many times before, and now, reinforced by his summer's training in the New Testament, he dove into the heated discussion feet first. Each debater quoted chapter and verse, only to be out-quoted by his opponent, followed by rebuttal, and then re-rebuttal... until something out of the ordinary happened.

A STEWARDESS led two weeping little boys up the aisle and Moish overheard her tell her co-workers the shocking news: the boys' father, who was seated in the rear of the plane, had just suffered a heart attack and the stewardess wanted to spare the children the anguish of seeing their father in that state.

The "No Smoking" sign flashed on and the plane began to drop altitude. They were going to make an emergency landing in Newfoundland to let off the victim.

Oy vey, thought Moish. That poor man! And then suddenly remembered his own plight — now he would *surely* miss the flight to Vienna. But before he could absorb the implications of the situation, he heard one of the stewardesses — Betsy — tell her co-worker that the victim's wife, who by this time had become understandably hysterical, absolutely refused to deplane with her husband. She couldn't afford the additional air fare to get home.

"What can we do?" the girls asked each other helplessly.

How ironic, thought Moish, for this tragedy to arise just as he was in the midst of a dialogue on the subject of "practice what you preach." The priest repeatedly accused the Jews of being hypocritical and sanctimonious in this regard. It was Moish's turn to rebut, but instead he followed his natural instinct, bred of years of yeshiva-training. Grabbing his air-sickness bag, he excused himself and began marching down the aisle, addressing each of the charter group members in turn:

"Would you kindly open your hearts to our fellow passengers in their hour of need?" he asked, *proffering the bag.*

One by one, the passengers reached into their pockets and purses, all touched by the gesture. Coins and notes materialized from some of the most unlikely places, and all were tossed into the sick-bag.

"Are Marks alright?"
"Naturally, danke schoen."
"How about Francs?"
"Merci, merci, yes, of course."

The stewardesses, catching on to what was happening, virtually hugged each other from joy. One-third down the aisle, the bag could hold no more and Moish returned to the galley for some more sick-bags. He handed over his treasure to the jubilant stewardesses, who quickly emptied the bag and began counting the donations. Fellow passengers volunteered to assist with the collection, but Moish was unwilling to share this *kiddush Hashem*. As he returned down the aisle, Betsy announced over the P.A. system:

"Ladies and gentlemen, may I have your attention please. So far we have $521 – 60 Marks, 49 Pounds Sterling, and 220 Francs. Thank you all!"

THE PASSENGERS were wonder-struck. The contributions were so spontaneous and genuine: it was their first encounter with the beauty of *tzeddaka*. A Hare Krishna pulled out his beat-up guitar and composed an instant hymn about giving. It was 2:15 in the morning, but everyone was wide awake, clapping, humming, and donating.

"Ladies and gentlemen, we have another $250 – 100 Francs and 60,000 Lire, and we're still counting!"

The announcement generated an atmosphere charged with the excitement of a telethon with the passengers as the stars. The goal of $800 was soon reached and the money ceremoniously presented to the wife of the heart attack victim. She wanted to embrace the abashed yeshiva *bochur*, who politely declined the honor. Moish calmly returned to his seat beside a crimson-faced priest, who couldn't bring himself to lift his gaze from his lap. With a twinkle in his eye, Moish asked:

"I'm sorry, sir, I forgot. What was it you were saying? Something about hypocrisy?"

Fortunately for the priest, before he could answer — not that he even knew *what* to answer — the pilot emerged from the cockpit, and all eyes focused on the front of the plane.

"*Young man,*" he addressed Moish in his booming voice, "*I want to congratulate you. You've done a mighty big deed. Betsy here tells me you're worried about having missed your connecting flight to Vienna. Well, you don't have to concern yourself with that! Hungarian Airlines has just inaugurated a Friday afternoon flight and I radioed ahead – they're holding the plane for you!"*

Nodding his gratitude, Moish was speechless at the *Hashgacha Pratis*, (Divine Providence), and sat down to continue studying for his *farheir*.

"I told Dad not to worry. ."

UP UP AND A...VEY!

> *Hashgacha Pratis (Divine Providence) refers to God's guiding hand in every aspect of human endeavor. The protective canopy of Hashgacha Pratis shed over the Jewish people is often only recognized in a historical perspective and not perceived in daily life.*

WHEN RABBI BENZION Ehrlanger arrived at the KLM departure terminal in New York, he could already hear the Rosh Hashanah *nigunnim* humming through his head. Everything seemed in order; the flight to Athens was scheduled to leave on time and his flight Athens-Tel Aviv was confirmed. The anxiety of flying to *Eretz Yisrael* just two days before Rosh Hashanah coupled with last minute packing had kept him up all night. Just to make sure that his rest would not be disturbed, he selected a seat in the rear of the plane. It was September, 1975.

Rav BenZion Ehrlanger is a *ben shmonim* with a long white beard. He has *payos* tucked behind his ears, wears a frock (long black coat) and a large oval homburg which *roshei yeshiva* customarily wear. He looks unmistakably Jewish.

DING DONG: "First call for KLM Flight 739 to Athens now boarding Gate 42."

Rav Ehrlanger grabbed his bag and fumbled for his boarding card sandwiched between his *Tehillim* and

Chumash. Boruch Hashem, thank God, he sighed. A delayed takeoff could cause him to miss his connecting flight, and with Rosh Hashanah just forty hours away, there was no time to spare.

The thrill of takeoff and seeing New York aglow at night was of little interest to Rav BenZion. All he wanted was to shut his eyes, but first he instructed the steward to wake him when they landed in Athens. "Remember," he entreatingly repeated...

Rav Ehrlanger was still sleeping when the "no smoking-fasten your seat belt" sign flicked on.

"Hello. This is Captain Pool speaking, we'll be landing at Olympic International Airport in another twenty-five minutes. The temperature in Athens is 22° centigrade and overcast. The Aegean Sea is now visible from the left side of the plane. Please return to your seats and obey the no smoking sign."

WHEN RAV BENZION finally woke up it was three-quarters of an hour after takeoff from Athens. The flight steward, realizing his oversight, was bereft of speech.

..."Ah...Sir, you overslept..."
"You mean we're past Athens?"
"And how!"
"Can't we return to let me off?"
"Impossible."
"But it is Rosh Hashanah eve and I must be in Israel for Rosh Hashanah. Is the next stop close to Israel?"
"Geographically..., yes."
"Where is it?"
"Beirut, Lebanon."
"LEVANOIN! *Ribbono Shel Olam!*"

When the plane landed in Beirut, Rav Ehrlanger was instructed by the crew not to disembark. After all the passengers had departed, a steward handed Rav BenZion a blanket and advised him to cover himself lest he be spotted from a window. The blanket also helped envelop his heart which was thumping so loudly he was afraid it would alarm the authorities.

After a little while, which seemed to take forever, new passengers began to board the plane. Rav Ehrlanger fervently prayed that he would be able to spend *yom tov* among Jews — or at least on the ground. He had already crossed three time zones and was helplessly losing the fight against time. It was difficult to muster the courage to ask what the next destination was. On the other hand, what could be worse than Beirut?

> *"Good morning ladies and gentlemen. This is your Captain speaking. We hope to takeoff any minute, please fasten your seat belts and obey all instructions. We will be flying at an altitude of 32,000 feet and will arrive in Bombay at 11:00. We hope you have a pleasant flight."*

Bombay, India! This was going to be a memorable Rosh Hashanah, not that Rav Ehrlanger was looking for memories. At least he would be on the ground before *yom tov*... or so he hoped.

About half an hour before the plane was due to land the captain made the following announcement:

> *"Ladies and gentlemen: I regret to inform you that due to civil disobedience which has just erupted over election irregularities, no flights are being allowed to land in Bombay. India has shut her borders. We have received landing rights in Bangkok, where we will arrive in another two and a half hours."*

After having spent the war years with the Mirrer Yeshiva in Shanghai, Bangkok didn't phase Rav BenZion — at least from a locational point of view. The situation at hand, however, was considerably more complicated.

After landing, he immediately inquired at the information desk if there was a synagogue or Jewish community in town. To his grateful astonishment, there was a synagogue in Bangkok and it wasn't too far from the airport. Rav Ehrlanger hailed a taxi and arrived at the synagogue minutes before sunset.

JEWS HAVE lived in Bangkok for at least a century, with several European families laying claim to several generation's worth of ancestors. During the Vietnam war, there was a large U.S. military presence in Thailand and Jewish Air Force chaplains officiated at weekly services. Today, the Jewish community consists primarily of American and Israeli diplomats, U.N. personnel and executives of international corporations. Together with those families who hold Thai citizenship, their number hardly exceeds a hundred souls. Such clientele doesn't call for an orthodox synagogue, and the seating of men and women was mixed.

Rav BenZion's sudden arrival at the synagogue was like an apparition appearing out of the sky. *Meshulochim* (solicitors) from yeshivos never made it to that neck of the woods. The president of the synagogue, Mr. Isaac Tresser, offered to be Rabbi Ehrlanger's host, and was able to dig up a box of American Goodman matzos and some cans of gefilte fish which met with the Rabbi's approval.

Praying posed a serious problem. Unwilling to participate in a mixed-pewed service, Rabbi Ehrlanger prayed in a small room adjacent to the sanctuary. When it came time for the Torah reading, Rav BenZion entered to listen.

Directly afterwards, he asked permission from the president to speak to the congregation. He was awarded the podium and aptly chose "The Sanctity of the Synagogue and Jewish Education," for the topic of his sermon.

A little unrehearsed at speaking to such an audience, not to mention ignorance in the art of tact, Rav BenZion got straight to the point. "You know why I am not praying with you? Because without a *mechitzah* (separation between men and women), this simply isn't a synagogue!"

The congregants turned in dismay to their rabbi, a Reform chaplain from the U.S. Army. He assured them that the *mechitzah* went out with Shabbos and kashrus a long, long time ago.

Rabbi Ehrlanger concluded his sermon by saying that without a *mechitzah* he would not be able to remain and pray with them. And sure enough, when he saw that the Reform rabbi refused to accommodate, he got up to leave. Dr. Frankel, a prominent congregant, arose from his seat and asked, "What difference does it make if we separate ourselves and allow this rabbi to remain?" "That's right!" "Why not?" was heard and the congregants proceeded to divide.

Actually, the synagogue was still unsanctioned by *halacha* for it lacked an actual *mechitzah,* but its current appearance was somewhat commendable. The absence of a *mechitzah* prevented Rav Ehrlanger from actually praying with the congregation, but in order to demonstrate his approbation, he pretended to participate and joined in the recital of the *Kaddish.*

At the conclusion of services an amazing thing occurred. Some young people approached Rav BenZion and said, "Rabbi, you mentioned *teshuva,* yeshiva, learning... in your sermon — we don't even know what these words mean." With a gleam in his eyes, Rav Ehrlanger responded, "There is a yeshiva for you in Jerusalem..."

Not much later Josef Tresser arrived via Thailand at the Ohr Somayach Yeshiva in Jerusalem. He was the first of several students *cum-ba'alei teshuva* to arrive and change their lives in wake of this sleepy *erev* RoshHashanah mishap.

REB HIRSH MICHEL'S YERUSHALAYIM SHEL MA'ALAH

Yerushalayim Shel Ma'alah is not a geographic location. The Midrash relates that there is a heavenly Jerusalem beyond man's farthest ken of Divinity in congruence with the earthly Jerusalem. The celestial angels who make up the Jerusalem above found their counterparts in the Jerusalem below one hundred years ago, when amongst humble tinsmiths and cobblers were pious individuals who spent the major part of their days engaged in spiritual pursuits. The paragon of tzidkus and yirah of this saintly generation was Rabbi Yehoshua Zvi* Michel Shapiro.

THE RAIN POURED down so hard that night, that the well-trodden streets of "Battei Machse" were rivulets. In the midst of the storm, the door to the Sephardi *shul*, Chessed El, opened to a cobblestone alley. It was an hour after midnight, in November 1868.

Battei Machse, in the heart of the old *yishuv*, was fast asleep. The few who might have ventured out at this hour remained at home, for the downpour posed a double threat. In addition to the obvious health hazard, there was fear of the Turks who incarcerated in the dreaded Akishle prison

---

* "Zvi" translates in Yiddish as Hirsh (deer); hence Reb Hirsh Michel.

anyone caught out at night without a lit candle — no matter what the weather.

The door to the *shul* closed, and a man emerged with clothes draped over his head and shoulders. He wasn't carrying a candle — he never did. The clothes were not to protect him from the rain, but to protect his identity. Every night at an hour after midnight, he made this trip checking every corner to see if anyone was there.

Reb Hirsh Michel was on his way to his *chavrusa*. His every step and every act was veiled in secrecy. But the little that we do know about him — he was described as "The Yerushalimer Tzaddik" — is a portal to *Yerushalayim Shel Ma'alah*.

R EB HIRSH MICHEL's penchant for holiness was apparent at an early age. When he was eight years old he tasted his first apricot. The sweet, juicy savor, the pungent aftertaste and the soft peel made his mouth water. In sparcely stocked Palestine anything mildly saccarine or candied was a treat. He found its surprising sweetness and succulence so delectable that he considered the fruit an indulgence, and abstained from eating any for the rest of his life.

At the age of seven, he completed *Babba Metziah* in just a few nights, obviously comprehending it well. The *Ravad* (head of the *Beis Din* of Hevron), Rav Shimon Menashe, and the other local rabbinic luminaries enjoyed discussing Torah subjects with the young prodigy, but Hirsh Michel avoided such encounters. He felt that too much time was wasted in both discussion and travel, and only consented to meet with the elder scholars on fast days when his concentration was weak.

One afternoon, a merchant outside the Hevron Synagogue heard painful wails emanating from inside the shul. *He dropped his wares to try to be of help, but found the synagogue door locked. Convinced, nonetheless, that he had indeed heard moans, the merchant scaled the window railing but couldn't see a thing inside. He then heard another shrill cry which grew louder and longer. He summoned the shamash who unlocked the shul door and found the little feet of nine year old Hirsh Michel protruding from behind the paroches.*

Fearing discovery, Hirsh Michel covered his face and ran outside. "Someone must be ill in the Shapiro home," the men reasoned. To their astonishment, however, they discovered that everyone was well. Hirsh Michel had been pouring out his heart over the Temple which lay in ruin, imploring the Almighty to hasten its restoration.

W HEN HIRSH MICHEL was eleven, he heard about Reb Yisrael Salanter for the first time from a Lithuanian immigrant. Stories about Reb Yisrael and the nascent *"Mussar* Movement" so inspired the youngster that he made his first request from his father, Reb Yaakov Koppel — the purchase of the *mussar* classic *Mesilas Yesharim*. His father acceded to the request and had the *nachas* of seeing his son memorize and embody its each and every word.

At age 17, Hirsh Michel married the daughter of the famous *ga'on*, Rabbi Nachman Nosson Koronell. After his marriage he returned to Jerusalem which he had left for Hevron as a young boy to study under Rabbi Yosef Steinhart (Rav Yosef *"Charif"* — the Sharp One), a nephew and disciple of Reb Chaim Volozhiner.

The Torah giants of Jerusalem flocked to greet Reb Hirsh Michel, but he tried to avoid them. Reb Hirsh Michel had moved to Jerusalem to study undisturbed, not to be a center of attention. His desire to study by himself, however, was soon to change.

NOT LONG after Reb Hirsh Michel's return to Jerusalem, Rabbi Moshe Yehudah Leib, the *Ga'on MiKutna* — the Rav of Kutna, Lithuania (who was succeeded by the celebrated Reb She'ala) also arrived. The *Ga'on* MiKutna became the local focal point of Torah study. Jerusalem's *talmidei chachamim* spent a good part of their day in his home involved in Talmudic discussions; and only Reb Hirsh Michel remained in the *beis midrash*. He viewed stepping outside, even to discuss Torah intricacies, a waste of time. His daily schedule consisted of learning an entire *mesechta* with all of the commentaries every day, plus ten folios from a different *mesechta*, in addition to his lengthy *mussar* studies. In fact, he never would have met the Kutna Rav had his father not insisted that he present himself to him.*

It did not take the *Ga'on* MiKutna long to realize that this young man was superior to the other scholars and was worthy of his undivided attention. The elderly Rav felt duty bound to impart all of his knowledge to this exceptional student, and later quoted him extensively in his works, *Zayis Ra'anon* and *Tiferes Yerushalayim*. Reb Hirsh Michel also wrote several letters explicating and defending the words of his *rebbe*.

---

* In 5659 (1899), when the German Kaiser visited Jerusalem, Reb Hirsh Michel was caught in a similar dilemma: should he join the rest of the town in going out to recite the rare blessing "*Shechalak*," which is said upon seeing a monarch, or continue learning in seclusion? His difficulty was solved when a bottle of boiling water smashed on the floor and scalded his legs. He thanked God for this omen and joyfully returned to his studies, absolved from any obligation to bless the king.

AFTER THE PASSING of the *Ga'on* MiKutna in 1866, Reb Hirsh Michel returned to his old practices. Every night immediately after *Maariv,* he slipped away to the sparsely-attended Sephardi synagogue, Chessed El, for a long night of prayer and study. The few Sephardim in the *shul* were sure that this man was *Eliyahu Hanavi.*

He would gently place his cane on the table where people were learning and ask them to rap him on his fingers if he would doze off. He would then repair to a corner where he studied from a *Shulchan Aruch Choshen Mishpat,* which he held in his hands. With his sweet voice, he rapidly read through the text with *Shach, Taz,* and other commentaries, occasionally repeating a phrase or two. So he studied, standing perfectly still, hour after hour, night after night, never requiring the cane to keep him awake.

One night, however, Reb Hirsh Michel's eyelids began to droop... The others in the *beis hamidrash* felt themselves unworthy of disturbing such a saint, and did not dare touch him. When he awoke after a few evanescent minutes he was so pained by his drowsing that he trembled, his eyes ablaze. He tightened his fingers around the *Shulchan Aruch* as if to say, "Who knows what spiritual heights I forfeited by just these few minutes?" He took the people to task: "Why do I need a cane if it isn't going to be used?" — and then resumed his learning with fiery diligence.

REB HIRSH MICHEL never slept for an extended period of time, never after midnight, nor did he ever lie on a bed. Every night at an hour before midnight he rested his head against the wall while still standing and instructed those nearby not to allow him to sleep for more than ten minutes. He would always awake by himself, wash his hands and return to learning as before until exactly midnight. Reb Hirsh Michel then hurried to a *mikvah,* immersed himself and returned to the *shul.* He tilted his hat over his eyes, removed his shoes, placed ashes on his forehead and sat on the cold stone floor to say *Tikun Chatzos*.

Each word of the *Tikun* was said with transcendent fervor bemoaning the absence of the Divine Presence, the destroyed Temple, the *Sifrei Torah* that were burnt, the death of *tzaddikim*, the desecration of God's name, the exiles, the growth of Reform, as well as other aspects of *galus*. Reb Hirsh Michel mourned each loss as if it were his own personal tragedy, until the floor was wet from his tears. When he completed the *Tikun*, he put on his shoes and returned to the corner, remaining erect and engrossed in his studies until sunrise when he *davened* every morning.*

> *On an erev Shabbos in 5643 (1883), Reb Hirsh Michel appeared to be on the brink of death. The doctors of Jerusalem conferred at his bedside and decided that his only hope for recovery was an immediate operation. Reb Hirsh Michel calmly asked if that would affect "making Kiddush" in the evening. They replied that Kiddush or any other such activity would be out of the question for the next three days. "If I can't make Kiddush," he declared, "then I don't need an operation!"*
>
> *The following morning the doctors examined him and to their utter amazement found that his condition had totally improved and he no longer needed surgery.*

In 5663 (1903) Reb Hirsh Michel fell mortally ill and again Jerusalem's doctors visited him. Their consensus was that Reb Hirsh Michel's condition was fatal and they prohibited

---

* Nothing could alter Reb Hirsh Michel's vigorous daily schedule. When one of his children died early one Shabbos morning, he left his home to a neighbor's house where he learned the entire day without interruption as if nothing had happened. When it turned night and the laws of mourning which were suspended on Shabbos resumed he returned home and just then did people find out what had happened.

him to learn or exert himself in any way. When the doctors left, he began to cry and called for his student, Rabbi Yaakov Moshe Charlap. He asked Reb Yaakov Moshe to read to him the *Ran* at the beginning of *meseches Pesachim*.

"*But you are not allowed to learn*," Reb Yaakov Moshe protested.

"*If I am really going to die*," Reb Hirsh Michel responded, "*then when am I going to learn if I don't learn now?*"

And so they studied all that day and deep into the night, Reb Yaakov Moshe totally forgetting that his *rebbe* was sick.

One Succos, Reb Hirsh Michel fainted in his succah, and appeared to be minutes away from death. Crowds immediately gathered to pray on his behalf while his students struggled to revive him. After finally arousing him, they tried to carry him into his home where they could provide better care, but Reb Hirsh Michel refused to budge. Rabbi Yehoshua Leib Diskin (known in Jerusalem as the Brisker Rav) ruled that Reb Hirsh Michel was not to be listened to, and was to be brought into the house at once... Years later he explained, "I was afraid that I was at the very end of my life. How could I depart from the precious mitzva of sitting in the succah with just minutes left to live?"

For a time, Reb Hirsh Michel was advised to wear a pouch of hot stones to ease intestinal pain. His concentration was so intense during *davening* that one *Shacharis* a burning coal which was placed unwittingly amongst the stones ignited the entire pouch. In spite of smoke emitting from his clothing, he was oblivious to what was happening. Only when he finished *Pesukei DeZimrah* did he discover that he had sustained a third degree burn.

On another occasion, he did not realize that a hornet had stung him while he was *davening Shemona Esrei*, even though his neck was swollen and red.*

R<small>EGARDING</small> THE Talmudic dictum: "Whoever has enough bread for today and questions what he will eat the next day is a small believer" (*Sotah* 48), Reb Hirsh Michel** used to comment: "A *kotton amanna,* a small believer, is an *apikorus kotton...*"

The *Gemorah* relates that many failed who tried to live by Rav Shimon Bar Yochai's system of exclusively learning and forgetting about worldly pursuits. Reb Hirsh Michel added, "If many tried and failed, this implies that a few succeeded. Is there anything wrong with striving to be among that minority?!"

Reb Hirsh Michel fasted frequently. Otherwise his diet consisted of a piece of bread, which he measured to be

---

* This concentration was present in all of his pursuits. In 5627 (1867) he mounted a donkey to take him to a village near Jerusalem to oversee the wheat harvest in preparation for matzos. When he reached the village the donkey driver tapped Reb Hirsh Michel, who was engrossed in the *sugya* of עביד אינש דינא לנפשיה to demount. Reb Hirsh Michel remained absorbed in his thoughts while the donkey driver kept hitting and shoving him beyond the point of disgrace. Seeing that this was of no avail he started screaming and shouting, but this too couldn't disconcert him. Finally, in desperation, the donkey driver hauled Reb Hirsh Michel to the ground, and after about ten minutes Reb Hirsh Michel finally remembered why he had gotten on the donkey in the first place.

** Reb Hirsh Michel viewed the Rama's ruling (*Yoreh De'ah* 246), that one may not worry about the morrow, as the very foundation of Jewish life.

exactly a *k'beitzah* (an egg-size, the minimum for a blessing over washing the hands) dipped into oil, and a glass of unflavored hot water.

> *His students were once curious as to why he was in an exceptionally good mood. He explained that he had fasted that day because he had nothing to eat. He continued: "There are two opinions in the Gemorah as to whether one who fasts is a sinner or a pious individual. I have fasted by default, and have therefore avoided this dispute."*

REB HIRSH MICHEL guarded his private life zealously. When his father, Reb Yaakov Koppel, died in 5652 (1892), Rabbi Yehoshua Leib Diskin asked Reb Hirsh Michel to succeed his father as the head of the Suvalk *Kollel*. This placed him in a terrible dilemma. The very notion of accepting a public position that required so much social interaction was contrary to his chosen way of life. On the other hand, how could he refuse Reb Yehoshua Leib?

Reb Hirsh Michel secretly engaged ten men to join him at the *Kosel Hama'aravi* where he went daily to pour out his heart over the Temple's destruction and the *Shechina*'s absence. There they prayed fervently that Reb Yehoshua Leib would retract his offer.

Reb Hirsh Michel preserved even his most ordinary actions from the public eye — whether on his way to perform a mitzva, or simply going to the *Kosel*, he deliberately tried to mislead people as to where he was going. Every *erev Rosh Chodesh* after *Maariv*, Reb Hirsh Michel walked to *Kever Rochel*, in Bethlehem. He would arrive before midnight, and at *chatzos* he would say the entire *Sefer Tehillim*, and then head back for Jerusalem with added vigor and inspiration. He always returned in time for the sunrise *minyan*, showing no signs of exhaustion or tiredness from this grueling trek.

One *erev Rosh Chodesh*, Reb Hirsh Michel allowed a young man to accompany him, on the condition that no one else join them. They were engaged in a deep discussion of *mussar* until they encountered another man, also going to *Kever Rochel*. Reb Hirsh Michel dropped back, allowing the other two to continue ahead. After a ways, the young man noticed that Arabs were hurling rocks at Reb Hirsh Michel who was all by himself. He ran to Reb Hirsh Michel's aid, and apologized profusely for leaving him behind: "I had no choice," he pleaded. "The man who joined us is a stranger from abroad. It seemed appropriate to befriend him."

"You behaved properly," Reb Hirsh Michel responded, "but the mitzva didn't require my involvement. Had I remained, I would have had to interrupt my thoughts every minute to answer his questions about 'what is this?' and 'what is that?' Answering all of these questions would have hindered my concentration and violated Rabbi Yaakov's ruling, (*Avos* 3:7) 'He who is walking by the way and studies, and interrupts his study and exclaims: How beautiful is this tree! How fine that field! forfeits his life.' Therefore, I never travel with strangers."...(Because when was Reb Hirsh Michel *not* studying on the way?)

REB HIRSH MICHEL maintained the same secrecy in his writings as he did in his private life. He was determined to publish his manuscripts, which he considered to contain genuine Torah truths. This assumption, he felt, was supported by an omen: his entire cellar was once gutted by a fire, save a large box of his works. Notwithstanding this iron desire, he would only consent to their printing if they were to be published anonymously. And even when this stipulation was met, he rewrote them for publication quoting extensively from *Rishonim* and *Achronim* to make his original thinking appear as if it were simply an anthology.

Leaders of the Sephardi *kehilla* once approached Reb Hirsh Michel for a letter encouraging the saying of *Tikun*

Chatzos. He produced a major treatise, outstanding in brilliance and fear of heaven. How did he protect his identity? By writing the entire manuscript into Rashi script so that the courier would neither understand it nor be able to trace its origin.

When Reb Hirsh Michel received the first galleys he objected to the chapter title התעוררות לאהבת ישראל (arousal to love fellow Jews) for fear that people would be able to identify who actually wrote it. To further disguise his authorship, Reb Hirsh Michel quoted verbatim numerous Sephardi *sefarim* throughout the book. He also saw to it that the text of the *Tikun Chatzos* was printed together with his lengthy work, so that he could entitle the entire volume "*Tikun Chatzos*" — and exclude the author's name.

Several *sefarim* were steered into Reb Hirsh Michel's hands before publication. He wrote detailed, lengthy addenda and corrections to them, which were published in conjunction with the original work without the author or the public ever finding out who was behind it.

> Another example of his distaste for recognition was in 5659 (1899), when two brothers in Bombay sent a query to Rabbi Y.S. Alisher of Jerusalem: They were fighting over an inheritance and would only accept a ruling decided by the "Chacham Bashi," chief rabbinical authority. Rav Alisher refused to issue a decision unless Reb Hirsh Michel would attach his signature to the responsa. This simple request presented tremendous anguish to the overly modest Reb Hirsh Michel who finally acquiesced – signing the document just: "Zvi ben Yaakov" instead of his full name, seeing no other way out of helping the brothers.

THE LAST SIX years of Reb Hirsh Michel's life were plagued with a painful, debilitating disease... On Thursday,

9 Elul, 5666 (1906), after saying *Tikun Chatzos,* Reb Hirsh Michel returned home, very weak. Despite his faintness he tried to prepare himself for the morning prayers — to no avail. Blood started rushing from his head and exhaustion wrung his body. Reb Hirsh Michel collapsed.

He awoke just as the first streams of light diffused over *Har Habayis* — the Temple Mount. His attendants had just arrived and he motioned them to don him in his *tallis* and *tefillin.* Reb Hirsh Michel tried to concentrate so that he could pray at sunrise as usual, but he could barely move his lips. Somehow, despite it all, he mustered the strength and even stood for the *Shemona Esrei.*

After *davening,* an attendant brought him a drink of water, but he could not even murmur the blessing. He motioned for the attendant to say the *bracha* for him and he drew the cup to his lips. After numerous attempts, it was clear that he was not able to swallow.

The news broke instantaneously. Early that Thursday morning, every Yeshiva and Talmud Torah in Battei Machse was storming the gates of heaven with their prayers and *Tehillim,* and delegations were dispatched to all of the holy places to offer prayers on Reb Hirsh Michel's behalf.

On Friday his flagging condition deteriorated even more. Nevertheless, when Reb Hirsh Michel saw the dark of the night dissipate he gestured to bring over his *tallis* and *tefillin.* At *Shacharis,* a *shamash* had to turn the pages of the *siddur* for him.

As evening approached, his attendants changed his clothing into the all-white apparel he customarily wore on Shabbos. Although literally on his death-bed, he somehow gathered the stamina to pray standing up for the first three and the last three blessings of the Friday night *Shemona Esrei.*

After *davening,* his students carried him to the dining table where someone made *Kiddush* for him. He made several unsuccessful attempts at tasting the wine. The students then rolled up his sleeves to wash his hands, one of them making a blessing on his behalf. At *"Hamotzi,"* Reb Hirsh Michel could not even move his teeth. They tried dipping bread crumbs into the soup so that it would be easy to swallow — but this also was of no avail. Desperate to perform at least one mitzva at the Shabbos table, Reb Hirsh Michel motioned for his *siddur*. At every Sabbath meal he sang *Askinu Seudasa*: "Prepare the feast of perfect faith... pepare the feast of the king... this is the feast of... the Presence... come feast with it... קריבו שושבינין, עבידו תקונין, לאפשא זינין Draw near, beloved scholars, make preparations to multiply delicacies, fish and fowl, thereby creating holy souls above and new spirits below..." He glanced into the siddur for a few seconds, his eyes welled with tears and then hinted for them to carry him back to bed.

Shabbos morning Reb Hirsh Michel remained in bed asking for neither his *tallis* nor his *siddur*. Everyone in Jerusalem now knew how serious the situation was... After Shabbos he gathered his last ounce of faltering strength and gestured to make his last will. Those present could not understand what he wanted, and this afflicted Reb Hirsh Michel with even more pain.

Sunday morning, *Parshas Ki Savo,* a doctor examined him and summoned his students to come at once. All of Jerusalem poured into Battei Machse. The hats of the men and the *tichels* of the women formed a collage of black which covered the entire plaza. A *chazzan* led the crowd in responsive *Tehillim* on behalf of the *"Yerushalimer Tzaddik,"* while *minyanim* were dispatched to the *Kosel* and other sacred places.

The lines of *Tehillim* resounded like artillery shells bouncing off the stone walls and Valley of *Gehinnom* below. After hours of *Tehillim*, the *chazzan* suddenly fell silent. The sea of humans started breaking into waves to allow an old man wearing a black silk robe to get through.

Ninety year old Rabbi Shmuel Salant, the venerable "Rav of Jerusalem", who no longer set foot out of his own house, let alone all the way to Battei Machse, had also come to participate in the prayers. Reb Shmuel instructed those present to join him in changing Reb Hirsh Michel's name to "Yehoshua Zvi Michel *Chaim*."

> "*O trustful Healer, send recovery and compassion, kindness and mercy to the poor spirit and soul of Yehoshua Zvi Michel Chaim ben Raitzeh Golda; spare him from death, invigorate and strengthen him in accord with our beseechment... Even if it has been decreed in Your Beis Din Tzedek that he die from this illness, changing his name can alter the decree. He is no longer who he was; just as his name was changed so also may his verdict be changed from strict law to clemency, from death to life, from illness to a complete recovery me'atta ve'ad olam, Amen selah!*"

... But it was too late. Jerusalem's greatest scholars and *tzaddikim* had all packed into the Shapiro home. With broken hearts and unmatched fervor, they said *Shir Hamaalos* as their tears drowned out their cracked voices. With the awful realization that they were losing their master, they cried out "*Shema Yisrael*," "*Hashem Hu HaElokim*," "*Aleinu Leshabei'ach*" — and the earth tore asunder. At high noon the sun dimmed, and the great light of Israel was extinguished.

On 12 Elul, 5666 (1906), the Sephardi and Ashkenazi Rabbis issued a moratorium on work in Jerusalem, and all *yeshivos* and *chadorim* were dismissed, to attend the *tzaddik*'s funeral.

WHILE PREPARING Reb Hirsh Michel's body for the funeral, a strange copper key was discovered in his hand. No one had ever seen it before or had any idea which door it unlocked.

One person present remembered that when *Chacham* Sasson Persaido, the head of Beit El Chassidim Yeshiva

A Time to Embrace / 49

died, a similar copper key was found in his hand. "Rav Nachum Levi of Shadik," someone else recalled, "also had such a key on his body when he passed away." But then, too, its significance was a mystery.

When Rabbi Shmuel Salant made a condolence visit to the Shapiro home, he felt obliged to reveal exactly how great a loss Jewry had suffered with Reb Hirsh Michel's passing: "When the holy Rav Nachum of Shadik came across the *Midrash* that says that there is a special hidden place on earth where God moans His exiled Kingdom, he began to cry. If the Almighty has a specific place to weep over the *galus,* then certainly we too should designate a secret place to pray for the restoration of the Divine Kingdom.

"Adjacent to the Spring of Shiloach, where Rabbi Yishmael the High Priest used to immerse himself, is a skeleton structure within two inner courtyards, hidden from the public eye. Rav Nachum designated this ruin to be the hiding place of *Yerushalayim Shel Ma'alah,* and had a locksmith prepare a lock that could only be opened by special copper keys. These keys were entrusted to an elite group of men who had sanctified their bodies and purified their sight from an early age. In all of *Yerushalayim Shel Ma'alah*, only thirteen *tzaddikim* were deemed worthy of possessing such keys, and Rav Yehoshua Zvi Michel *Shapiro* זצוק'יל was the most deserving of all!"

REMEMBERING THE CHOFETZ CHAIM

> *The greatest way to catch a glimpse of a Torah giant and fathom the genius of his mind and soul is to relate his thoughts and actions. Perhaps no Torah personality has captured the hearts of so many Jews who wish to retell his every move as the "Chofetz Chaim." He lived in the small town of Radin, Poland, but word of his wisdom spread far and wide.*

IN ORDER to rescue a student who had been arrested for spying, the Chofetz Chaim agreed to travel to St. Petersburg and testify on his behalf. In Russian courts an affirmation is not accepted in place of a vow ("to tell the truth, the whole truth" etc.). The Chofetz Chaim, however, would not take an oath.*

To gain special permission for his client, the defense attorney related a story about the Chofetz Chaim to the judge: "This witness once invited a needy man off the street to lodge in his house. The guest, who was actually a criminal, robbed him of the available possessions and fled. The Chofetz Chaim ran after him, shouting, 'Don't worry, I shall not hold this against you. I grant you these items with a perfect heart...' "

---

*As an added stringency to the prohibition against swearing falsely some refrain from swearing altogether— even when the oath is the absolute truth.

"Tell me," asked the judge, "do you really believe this story?" "No, your honor, I don't," admitted the defense attorney, "but do they make up stories like this about you and me?..."

HALF A CENTURY after the Chofetz Chaim's passing, it is as if he never died. His name is quoted daily in the context of a *halacha,* story or parable. Such a host of stories have emerged about the Chofetz Chaim from those who knew him and had seen him, that it is truly unnecessary to make up stories about his greatness—his stature clearly overshadows our imagination. Even the tales which didn't happen could have, and many more did that we'll never know.

Despite the numerous scholarly works the Chofetz Chaim produced, he is remembered best as a folk hero. He considered himself one of the common people and never accepted the position of rabbi in his own town.

From a tender age he displayed signs of saintliness. As a youngster, every night he would empty the water buckets which had been filled by children playing a practical joke on the water boy. This way he spared the "water *shlepper*" hours every morning cracking the ice which would have formed in the buckets.

Four years after his marriage, the Chofetz Chaim received an inheritance of 150 rubles which enabled his wife to open a grocery store. He used to visit the store periodically to make sure that the measures and scales were kept clean and accurate. With perfect faith in God he wished to expend only the minimum effort on mundane pursuits and closed the store as soon as he had earned enough money to live for the day.

When he realized that because of his honesty

people were only patronizing his store and neglecting others he closed the operation entirely.

THE SCORES of stories told about the Chofetz Chaim, such as the time he tore up a postage stamp to reimburse the government for lost revenue because of a letter which had been delivered to him via courier or similar other accounts highlighting his honesty, kindness, responsibility and modesty pale, nonetheless, when compared to what is told about his most famous characteristic.

In his early thirties, the Chofetz Chaim launched a campaign against slander (*lashon hara*) and defamation. The backbone of what was to turn into an ethical revolution was a book he published anonymously entitled, *Chofetz Chaim,* from which he received his name. A verse in Psalm 34 asks: "Who is the man who desires life (*chofetz chaim*) and loves days to see good? Guard your tongue from evil and your lips from speaking guile..."

Imagine trying to write an essay about the evils of slander. Some might be hard-pressed to compose five paragraphs. The Chofetz Chaim produced a 300-page masterpiece. The cynicism and scorn which might have been expected to assail a man who lectured and wrote about the sin of gossip never surfaced. Numerous attempts to prove the author's own inability to refrain from slander invariably failed, showing not only that he was genuine, but that his sole motivation was to unite Jews and stop them from besmirching each other.

THERE IS, the story goes, only one law regarding *lashon hara* about which the Chofetz Chaim was unresolved. That one may not defame someone else, or even listen to gossip — be it true or false — was not up for question. But what about speaking badly about oneself? Surely this could not be slander? An incident finally brought the Chofetz Chaim to a decision on this point.

Once, on a trip out of town, he shared a coach with a Jew from a different city. As was his custom, the Chofetz Chaim tried to befriend his travelling companion:

> "Shalom aleichem! Who are you, where are you from and where are you headed?"
>
> "My name is ——, I am from ——, and I am going to hear the holy Chofetz Chaim speak." Unaware that he was addressing the sage himself, the traveller continued to extol him.
>
> "He really isn't all you make him out to be," the Chofetz Chaim assured him.
>
> "But what are you saying? Do you know who you are referring to?"
>
> "Yes, I know him very well, and I repeat, when you get to know him he isn't really that great."

The discussion continued until, finally, the Jew was unable to control his rage at the blasphemy and slapped the other in the face. By this time, the coach had arrived at its destination and hundreds of people thronged around it to greet the Chofetz Chaim. When his companion realized whom it was that he had hit, his shame was so great that from then on the Chofetz Chaim ruled that one may not even speak *lashon hara* about oneself.

HE WORE the same poor black coat every day. He kept a special silk one in his closet ready to be donned upon news of the *Moshiach's* arrival. The Chofetz Chaim's firm belief in the imminent coming of the *Moshiach*, which he spoke and wrote about in *Tzipisa Leyeshua* was reflected in more than just his wardrobe. His whole lifestyle emphasized that this world is ephemeral, and that true living only begins in the world to come.

An American Jew once visited the Chofetz Chaim at his home, in the small town of Radin, Poland. The visitor was amazed at how bare the furnishings were in the dwelling of so noted a sage. There was nothing but a simple table, benches and a bed. Astonished, he asked why there were no other furnishings or necessities.

The Chofetz Chaim replied with a soft question: "Tell me, where is your furniture?" More baffled than before, the visitor retorted, "I am simply a tourist on a trip, and am not stopping long in any one place. I need no furniture on such an excursion; it would only get in my way."

The Chofetz Chaim smiled. "I too am only a tourist, a mere traveller in this world, expecting to be here for just a short while. This world is only a vestibule before the world to come. For a vestibule, it is furnished quite adequately..."

THE CHOFETZ CHAIM'S descendants living in Jerusalem remember some other incidents and *hashkafah*s not commonly known about their father:

Luxuries were anathema to the Chofetz Chaim. Far greater an evil than the emphasis luxuries placed on this world was the amount of *bitul* Torah that they generated.

The Chofetz Chaim's second wife, Miriam Fraida*,

---

*This is his second wife. When she moved to Radin after the

was the daughter of a well-to-do rav, accustomed to a more comfortable existence than the sparse life style afforded her in Radin. The Chofetz Chaim's living room/dining room was furnished with just one long table, made out of unsanded wooden planks, and three plain backless benches.

One morning the Chofetz Chaim returned from *davening* to find four new chairs, the likes of which were never seen in Radin, adorning his living room. He was aghast. His wife explained that she was simply ashamed to sit distinguished visiting rabbis on a shabby bench.

"Would you ever allow someone to sit on a gemorah?" he asked. *"How am I to pay for these chairs? I'll have to sell more books to cover the expense which means running to the printer, looking after the binder, contacting the distributor... in short, it means hours and hours not spent learning. You are mistaken if you believe that you will finally be able to offer a guest a chair – in fact, you will be sitting him on a gemorah!*

Furthermore, the Almighty has declared that neither His name nor His throne shall be complete until Amalek will be destroyed. If God's throne is not complete, how can we sit on four perfect chairs?" To make sure that the point was understood the Chofetz Chaim continued discussing the matter for another eight or nine hours...

wedding, she told the Chofetz Chaim at the outset that she simply would not be able to live in a house with a dirt floor. Although disappointed, the Chofetz Chaim agreed to have a cheap wooden floor installed.

The same idea was demonstrated when the Chofetz Chaim found a *Korban Mincha siddur* in the hands of his newly-wed daughter. "What's this?" he asked. "Just a *siddur*," she responded, but there was no evading the Chofetz Chaim. "But why do you need such a thick *siddur* printed on such expensive paper with an elegant binding?" "I *daven* better from this *siddur*," she answered hoping that this pietistic explanation would conclude the discussion. But she again was mistaken.

"God," responded her father, "answers the prayers uttered from all *siddurim*. He doesn't care if they are embossed in gold or have a leather binding... But He does care that your husband will have to waste precious learning time to get the money to pay for it. Don't you realize that money is only gained at the expense of time that could be devoted to Torah study? You start with a *siddur* and then want silver candlesticks, and then curtains, and then you'll want the walls refurbished..."

The Chofetz Chaim continued speaking to her about this subject for no less than three hours until she finally confessed that all brides receive a *Korban Mincha siddur* from their husbands. Although she wanted to be like everyone else, after this discussion she offered to return it. The Chofetz Chaim suggested instead that they share the *siddur* and he paid his son-in-law half of the cost. Whenever the Chofetz Chaim travelled out of town, he took this *siddur* with him, to demonstrate that he was indeed a part owner.

THE CHOFETZ CHAIM did not restrict his plea for the uncompromising supremacy of Torah values to just his family, but expected those close to him to embrace the same standard. At a large gathering to promote *yeshiva ketanas*, the Chofetz Chaim was the keynote speaker. The meeting was attended by prominent *roshei yeshiva* and *rabbonim*, including Rav Chaim Ozer Grodzenski zt'l of Vilna, famed teacher and scholar. In the course of his delivery the Chofetz Chaim became so engrossed in his passionate plea that his student, Rav Elchonon Wasserman zt'l, had to interrupt and inform him that sunset was quickly approaching, and it was time to *daven Mincha*. Oblivious to the hint, the Chofetz Chaim continued speaking until Rav Elchonon signalled again that there were just a few minutes left until *shkia*.

Obviously disappointed with Rav Elchonon's lack of appreciation of the subject at hand, the Chofetz Chaim exclaimed, "We are dealing with matters of life and death to *Klal Yisrael*, and you have *Mincha* on your mind!..."

There is a lot to relate about the Chofetz Chaim that cannot be conveyed in a story: The Chofetz Chaim knew human nature well enough to distrust people and doubt the veracity of their tales. Not incidentally this must have helped him discount any *lashon hara* that he might have heard. "תמים תהיה עם ד׳ אלוקיך— be completely trusting in God," he used to say, "but not with people!"

HE WOULD OFTEN be more stringent in personal conduct than his own rulings required, to avoid desecrating God's name. At the end of his life, when he was clearly not required to spend Succos sleeping in a freezing *succah*, he would do so nonetheless, so that others who were truly obligated would not be lenient with themselves.

According to his own confession he never uttered an unnecessary blessing, mentioned God's name in vain or without cause, and adhered to *Takonas* Ezra (immersing in a *mikvah* before *davening*.)

The Chofetz Chaim insisted that his wife, Miriam Fraida, z'l, (who was also exceptionally imbued with *chessed*), not wash the floors. The Chofetz Chaim, it was known, was an immaculate individual in his personal cleanliness, and in his old age would not hesitate to bend down to pick up a scrap of paper off the floor. So why should his wife not mop the floor? He feared that a poor person, with mud on his boots, would not be graciously received in the house if the floor was just cleaned...

Nevertheless, the Rebbitzen washed the floors every morning when the Chofetz Chaim went out to pray and was unaware of what transpired at home. One morning the Chofetz Chaim came home in the middle of *davening* and caught his wife mopping the floor. Despite his ire, the Chofetz Chaim didn't raise his voice, he never did. The Chofetz Chaim had a different way of showing his displeasure: "Too bad, too bad," he cried to himself out loud, "If only people would scrub their *neshamah* instead of the floor— think how clean and pure they would be!"

Rebbitzen Zaks, the Chofetz Chaim's daughter, had one closing comment about the idea of writing stories about the Chofetz Chaim: "My father, z'l, wanted people to study his books, not him..."

But we see that as a reflection of his personal humility, that the values the Chofetz Chaim cherished live on in these stories as they do in his writings...

The Vision of Yechezkel

RABBI YECHEZKEL ABRAMSKY *zt"l* used to say that a person's life is like a book: the day of birth is the first page; the day of death, the last page. Each intermediate day is a separate page in the book that man is assigned to author. Reb Yechezkel (Chatzkal) Abramsky, who was born on 5 Adar, 5646 (1886), in the small town of Dashkovtse, near the Mosst district of Vilna, wrote a wondrous work that was 90 years long.

WHEN REB YECHEZKEL was only eight years old, he could quote entire chapters from *Tanach* by heart, to the delight of the Jews of Mosst. At seventeen, he left home to learn in Novardhok under the "*Alter*" — Rabbi Yosef Yoizel Horowitz. In less than a year, he received *smicha* from the Rav of Novardhok, Rabbi Yechiel Michal Epstein, author of the *Aruch Hashulchan*.

Reb Yechezkel left Novardhok to study in the Telshe yeshiva. Due to the unsuccessful revolution in Russia and the infamous army conscription, Telshe became isolated from the yeshiva world. Food was scarce and the yeshiva's only *sefarim* were *gemara*s and the *Chiddushei HaRashba*. Reb Yechezkel mastered them all.

His diligence was renowned even before his arrival in Telshe. He used to say that a *masmid,* a diligent student, is one who learns sixty minutes an hour. When his sister passed away, he told a group of *talmidei chachamim* who had come to console him of Reb Chaim Soloveitchik's explanation of the *Yerushalmi Moed Kattan:* "A mourner who is adamant that he learn Torah may do so during the period of mourning when Torah study is forbidden." A mourner is not permitted to study Torah because of the prohibition against joy, which study promotes. A mourner, however, is not required to inflict pain on himself. Therefore, one who is so obsessed with Torah study and actually aches in its absence, would be permitted to resume his study. The *talmidei chachamim* immediately told Reb Yechezkel that he may resume studying.

When Reb Yechezkel reached conscription age for the Czarist army, he was forced to leave Telshe for Vilna, the "Jerusalem of Lithuania." There he entered the Ramalies Yeshiva and became acquainted with Reb Chanoch Aigesh, author of the *Marcheshes.* Rav Aigesh was greatly impressed with the young Yechezkel Abramsky — so impressed that he recommended to his cousin, Rabbi Yisrael Yehonason Yerushalemsky, that he consider Reb Yechezkel as a suitable match for his daughter. And so, on *erev Rosh Chodesh* Tammuz, 5669 (1909), the couple were married in Eihuman.

AFTER REB YECHEZKEL HAD LIVED in the home of his father-in-law for a year and a half, Rav Yerushalemsky advised him to continue his studies under the famed Reb Chaim "Brisker" Soloveitchik. Reb Yechezkel followed the advice, and spent four months with Reb Chaim. It was an encounter which marked the start of a long and fruitful relationship, one that found expression in many areas, including Reb Yechezkel's own commentary on *Chiddushei Rabbeinu Chaim Halevy al HaRambam.*

Reb Yechezkel considered Reb Chaim's words of Torah to be definitive and always deferred to him in any dispute. He once related that after he had written a *chiddush* on the *Tosephta,* Reb Chaim appeared to him in a dream and urged, *"Min darf lernen mehr Torah"* (One must learn more Torah). As soon as he awoke, he reviewed his notes and found that the very *mishna* he had intended to use as a proof in support of his argument, in fact served as a refutation of it.

THE LUBAVITCHER REBBE, Rabbi Shalom Ber, invited Reb Yechezkel to be the *Rosh Yeshiva* of his Tomchei Temimim Yeshiva. The students were so enthralled by his lectures that they lingered long after the classes were over to discuss his ideas further. This resulted in their late arrival for the daily *Tanya* class. When the Lubavitcher Rebbe learned of this, he informed Reb Yechezkel that while his greatness in Torah was genuinely admired, he would be better suited to direct a different yeshiva.

The Rebbe advised the Chabad chassidim of Smolian to accept Reb Yechezkel as their Rabbi. On his second day in Smolian, he was asked his first *shailah* (halakhic query) — and for some reason he could not remember the ruling. This was a significant test for him as his reputation was at stake. He could easily have replied in an ambiguous manner, but his honesty compelled him to respond: "I don't know."*

---

* On one hot *shiva assar beTammuz* fast day, a man knocked on Reb Yechezkel's door to solicit charity for his daughter's wedding. Reb Yechezkel gave him his usual donation and later that evening found the

In 5674 (1914), Reb Yechezkel accepted the invitation to succeed Rabbi Avraham Duber Kahane (author of *Dvar Avraham*) as head of the prestigious community of Smolovitch. With the outbreak of World War I that year, Rabbi Chaim Brisker resettled in Minsk, a half-hour's train ride from Smolovitch. Reb Yechezkel adopted the custom of leaving Smolovitch for Minsk every Sunday and returning in time for Shabbos. For three consecutive years these trips continued and profoundly affected Reb Yechezkel's development as a *talmid chacham* and leader of *Klal Yisrael*.

R EB YECHEZKEL never discussed his plans to embark on writing his monumental work on the *Tosephta* (writings parallel to the *Mishna* under the redaction of Rav Hiyya and Rav Oshiya), the *Chazon Yechezkel,* with his rebbe. Nevertheless, one day Reb Chaim overheard Reb Yechezkel discuss a complex subject related to the *Tosephta* with Reb Chaim's son, Velvel (the Brisker Rav). "It is apparent from your words," he said, "that you intend to write a book on the *Tosephta* — a most necessary project." To Reb Yechezkel these words implied his rebbe's approval for what was to become his life's occupation.

[When his wife became ill, Reb Yechezkel contemplated delaying the publication of some of his manuscripts until a time when he was less anxious and could concentrate completely on his work. Reb Yechezkel employed the *Goral HaGra* to solve his dilemma, and when the *goral*

---

same man in the synagogue. Reb Yechezkel invited him to break the fast at his house, which was close by, and save walking back in the heat on an empty stomach. The offer was declined with the confession: "I didn't fast." When Reb Yechezkel heard this, he contributed even more money, saying, "Now I see that you are truly an honest man."

landed on the verse, "*Yizal mayim medalyo*" — water shall flow from His bucket (Bamidbar 24:7), he understood that publication should proceed as planned.]

The importance Reb Yechezkel attached to the *Chazon Yechezkel* is clear from his *tzava'a* (will), in which he instructed that his books be borne behind him at his funeral. He also promised to be an advocate in the Heavenly Court for anyone who studied from his books. Reb Yechezkel's intention was to introduce the *Tosephta* into the yeshiva curriculum: "Each and every *halacha* should be explained in a simple and clear manner according to the literal meaning of the words, rejecting any interpretations foreign to *halacha* and incompatible with what is written." (From the introduction to *Zeraim*.)

Despite the fact that the *Tosephta* is one of the primary sources for both Talmuds — *Yerushalmi* and *Bavli* — the *Tosephta* had never attained any popularity in yeshivos. The *Chazon Yechezkel* brought the *Tosephta* out of the crypt with a *bayur,* a terse explanation of the *Tosephta*'s words, and *chiddushim,* explanations of the *Tosephta* in light of the *gemara* and *Rishonim*.

AT THE END of World War I, the Jews continued to suffer persecution. In Smolovitch, where Reb Yechezkel was the Rabbi, the anti-Semitic Poles perpetrated countless atrocities, including the shaving off of Jews' beards by force. When the thugs arrived at Reb Yechezkel's house he exclaimed, "I am a Rabbi and a Rabbi must have a beard!" His bold response startled his assailants and they decided to leave him alone. Reb Yechezkel, however, was not content until he received an official document from the authorities prohibiting the removal of his beard. This heroic story quickly spread among the Jews and inspired countless others not to succumb to the ruthless intruders.

Following the Bolshevik Revolution in 1917, the position of the Jews in Russia deteriorated considerably. Even religious marriage was banned. Despite the great danger involved, when Rabbi Abramsky heard of a bride and groom who wished to be wed, he would invite them to his house where he would marry them in secret.

WHEN RABBI Issar Zalman Meltzer left Russia in 5683 (1923), the Jews of Slutzk asked Reb Yechezkel to replace him as their Rabbi. He served as the Rabbi of Slutzk, displaying great self-sacrifice for nearly seven years. Reb Yechezkel ensured that the sacred covenant of circumcision remained alive, and regularly gave part of his meager salary to the *mohel* in nearby Harazuva.*

Whenever a male child was born, Reb Yechezkel would visit the family and plead with them to have the baby circumcised, despite the danger. To facilitate this, he devised the following plan: The father would leave his house on the day of the *bris*. Rebbetzen Abramsky, laden with baskets from the market, would stop in front of the baby's house and remove her shoe. This was a sign to the *mohel*, following close behind, to enter and quickly perform the sacred ritual.

While in Slutzk, Reb Yechezkel joined with Rabbi Shlomo Yosef Zevin in publishing a Torah journal, *Yigdal*

---

* During his stay in Smolovitch, he donated a large portion of his salary to hire a man to discreetly inform the local Jews every *erev Shabbos* before sundown that, "The Shabbos Queen is approaching; it is time to close your shops."

Torah, which was outlawed by the Communist government after just two issues were published.

Reb Yechezkel was also a member of a rabbinical council partially sponsored by the Lubavitcher Rebbe, Rabbi Yosef Yitzhak Schneerson, dedicated to strengthening Jewish observance in Russia. The Soviet authorities considered Reb Yechezkel's membership in the council subversive and warned him repeatedly to stop all activities related to the council. They also refused to allow him to leave Russia in order to accept an invitation to become the Rabbi of Petach Tikva, after the passing of Reb Yisrael Abba Citron. From that moment on, Reb Yechezkel was in constant danger.*

AFTER TEN MONTHS of hiding — moving to Moscow, Leningrad and other places — he was apprehended on *erev Rosh Chodesh* Elul 5690 (1930). He was accused of trying to overthrow the Soviet regime and was imprisoned in Moscow's infamous Lubyanka prison. The accusation was based on his meeting with Rabbi Yeshaya Glazer, a member of a United States fact-finding mission, which was investigating the state of religious freedom in the Soviet Union. Several months earlier, fourteen leading rabbis had been arrested in Minsk on the same charge after meeting with Rabbi Glazer. Despite the fact that Reb Yechezkel did not utter a word during his meeting with Glazer, the prosecutor demanded the death penalty. Owing to outside pressure, the sentence was commuted to five years of hard labor in Siberia.

From the time of his arrest, Reb Yechezkel's life became

---

* Reb Yechezkel once left his congregation on *Hoshana Rabba* in order to spend *Shmini Atzeres* and *Simchas Torah* together with Rabbi Zevin. He confided to his host that he felt the "earth burning under his feet."

a nightmare. He suffered terrible tortures in the cellars of the secret police: "At first they tried to persuade me to confess and be absolved from punishment. When they saw that this was to no avail, they said that they had ways of eliciting confessions that no human could endure. I realized that they didn't want only my soul, but the souls of all the rabbis. I therefore declared: 'I do not doubt your ability to harm me. I know that you can cut out my tongue and chop off my hands if you wish, but you will never succeed in getting me to utter a falsehood or sign an untrue statement.'"

REB YECHEZKEL arrived in Siberia wearing lightweight clothing which was virtually useless in that climate. "Every morning," he once related, "in temperature that often plummeted to 40 degrees below zero, we were forced to take off our shoes and run barefoot in the snow. From this torture alone, men fell like flies. I looked toward heaven and cried, 'Master of the Universe, you have taught us that everything is in the hands of Heaven except cold and heat (*Kesubos* 30a). Cold and heat are in man's own hands since man can guard himself from the elements by donning a coat or removing a sweater. This reason, however, no longer applies to me, for these iniquitous captors not only fail to provide me with clothes but force me to remove whatever I am wearing. My obligation to guard my health, therefore, returns to You. So please protect me, O God, for I trust in You!'

"As a child," he continued, "my mother always bundled me up warmly due to my frailty, while in the midst of that freezing Siberian cold I never once took ill or even caught a cold!"

Reb Yechezkel's first job was sawing heavy logs. When he was unable to fill his quota, he was punished with the assignment of stringing frozen fish onto wire. It was a dangerous task: he could not string the fish without wearing gloves, but with gloves on he couldn't feel the needle or the wire. Enervated, he uttered the "*viduy*" confessional every time he held the wire in his hand. After several weeks he was transferred to the more monotonous but less hazardous job of slicing bread for all the prisoners.

Reb Yechezkel once related that for a time he found it difficult to say the *Modeh Ani* prayer. "Why should I thank the Almighty for 'restoring my soul within me' for another torturous day? What kindness is there in mercifully restoring my soul if I cannot worship You properly? Until I finally realized that '*rabba emunasecha*' — Thy faithfulness is great! I thank You for providing me with an additional day of faith — it is worth enduring all these tortures as long as I can continue living and having faith in God for an extra moment."

ALMOST ALL of the twenty-four volume *Chazon Yechezkel* was written when Reb Yechezkel was a destitute prisoner. Rabbi Zevin testified that the words of the *Tosephta* never left Reb Yechezkel's lips, even when he was slaving at the most strenuous labor. Reb Yechezkel wrote in the introduction to *Zeraim* that even during the difficult days of World War I and in the subsequent years under Bolshevik oppression, "I did not cease to study and delve into the words of the *Tosephta*. While mountains were humbled with fear of the enemy and the Torah deserters raged like the tempest, I found the study of the *Tosephta* to be my greatest delight."*

---

* Prior to Reb Yechezkel's incarceration in Siberia, he had the foresight to entrust the *Chazon Yechezkel* manuscripts to Michael Rabinowitz, who brought the work with him to *Eretz Yisrael*. The manuscripts were later forwarded to a relative of Reb Yechezkel's, Reb Alter Vernofsky, who published the first volumes together with an introduction which alluded to the Iron Curtain separating the work from its author. When Reb Yechezkel was freed from Siberia in 5692 (1931), and settled in London, the other volumes were finally published.

A good portion of his novellae were written on the scraps of paper rationed out to prisoners for rolling cigarettes and without the aid of references. Reb Yechezkel's happiest day throughout the terrible ordeal was the day the authorities allowed his wife to bring him a volume of the *Tosephta*. And whenever he managed to send a letter to one of his colleagues, he did not describe the tortures he was suffering — instead, he invariably wrote something related to the *Tosephta*.

Reb Yechezkel's imprisonment in Siberia sparked an outcry in the Jewish world to secure his release. On *erev Yom Kippur* 5692 (1931), he was finally freed.*

During Reb Yechezkel's incarceration in Siberia, Europe's leading rabbis added the name "Yosef" to Yechezkel in the hope that he would merit release, just as *Yosef Hatzaddik* was saved from the Egyptian prison. Reb Yechezkel always cited the verse, "Then Pharoah sent and called Joseph and they brought him hastily out of the dungeon," when discussing his release. According to the interpretation of the Sforno, "Every Divine salvation is done in an instant." When Reb Yechezkel was finally freed on *erev* Yom Kippur, he didn't even have time to tie his shoelaces.

After his release, Reb Elchonon Wasserman greeted him and related the following story: "That very *erev* Yom Kippur I was learning with the Chofetz Chayim when all of a sudden he exclaimed, 'The Bolsheviks did not succeed, the Bolsheviks did not succeed! They were forced to free the Rav of Slutzk' — and then the Chofetz Chayim resumed learning. I looked at the clock and later found out to my astonishment that you were freed at that very hour!"

---

* Reb Yechezkel's deliverance from Siberia was the result of tireless efforts of the *Gedolei Hador* and the unprecedented intervention of the German Counselor, H. Bruening, who arranged the release in exchange for six communists jailed in Germany.

IN 5692 (1931), Reb Yechezkel was appointed Rabbi of the Machzikei Hadass Synagogue in London. After serving for two years as Rabbi, he was invited by the United Synagogues to head the Central *Beis Din* of Great Britain. This *Beis Din* was the fountainhead of the British Jewish communities. Reb Yechezkel made his acceptance of the post contingent upon stipulations regarding conversions and standards of *kashrus*. When these conditions were finally met — after a year and a half of negotiations — he accepted the post.

A London butcher who opposed Rabbi Abramsky's new *kashrus* standards lodged an appeal in court, claiming that the edicts did not conform with the spirit of freedom and democracy in Britain. When Rabbi Abramsky was subpoenaed to appear in court to answer the claim, community leaders, familiar with his strong will and his outspokenness, beseeched him not to agitate the stately and composed British judges. Unimpressed, Reb Yechezkel entered the courtroom and declared in a raised voice, "Nothing can stand before the truth! Democracy was created to protect and serve the truth and cannot be relieved of this obligation. When a Jew orders kosher meat he means exclusively meat that a knowledgeable Torah authority has certified, and anything other than that is fraud. The man who has come to protest this simple truth has sinned twice over: he denies the foundation of truth and degrades democracy as if it were made to serve lies..." In his judgement, the judge noted that, "albeit this old tiger roared a roar this courtroom is not used to hearing, I must, nevertheless, unequivocally rule that he is correct." *

---

* Appearing in court on a different occasion the judge asked, "Who is the greatest rabbinic authority today?" Reb Yechezkel answered, "I am." Startled, the judge responded, "I thought you were a humble man." "Yes," continued the Rabbi, "but I am under oath."

Despite Reb Yechezkel's forceful nature, he was able to endure insults and accept abuse when necessary. During the period of World War II, a man whose allegiance to Judaism was, at best, tenuous, began beating his wife and refused to agree to a divorce. In order to guarantee his wife's misfortune and destine her to become an *agunah,* he converted to Catholocism. Reb Yechezkel, always anxious to save a Jewish daughter from misfortune, offered to speak to the convert.

The *meshumad* finally agreed to grant his wife a divorce, but after the *get* was delivered, the convert told his former wife to remain behind for he wished to settle some financial matters with her.

Had she remained behind, it would have violated the Rambam's opinion of *veshilchah* — that the woman must be sent out of the house. Reb Yechezkel feared that the *get,* so difficult to obtain, would be invalidated. The *meshumad* was incensed and he let loose a barrage of insults and curses at Reb Yechezkel and the Jewish people in general. Nevertheless, Reb Yechezkel controlled his anger to the point of Hillelian tolerance and remained silent but firm until his ruling was upheld. He later commented to his son that he was glad that he had remembered this Rambam when it was *halacha lema'aseh* and not just for his writings.

Reb Yechezkel's son related that he always stood behind his father on the *Yomim Noraim* in order to help him rise after he had gone down on his knees for *Kor'im.* One year during *Kor'im* Reb Yechezkel began to cry. "What was it that you were praying for," his son asked, assuming that Reb Yechezkel must be praying for success in Torah learning, for health and for sustenance, or perhaps that his sons should be *talmidei chachamim.* To his son's surprise, Reb Yechezkel replied: "I am praying that all the matzos baked under my supervision should be truly free of any *chometz.*" Years later, after moving to Israel, he confided that when he went down on his knees during *Kor'im,* he then prayed that the *Chinuch Atzmai* school systems should never lose their financial backing.

Reb Yechezkel's son also described how, during World War II, his father pressured a Jewish soldier to write a conditional *get* for his wife before he set out for combat. That way, if he failed to return, the *get* could be presented and his wife would be spared the tragedy of becoming an *agunah*. The soldier finally agreed, but only on condition that the *get* be delivered via a third party. Reb Yechezkel acquiesced and put the *get* in the safe of the London *Beis Din*. That night, London was mercilessly bombed by the Germans, and the *Beis Din* was extensively damaged. Two floors of the building were razed by the Civil Guard so that passersby would not be injured by the bombed-out, crumbling structure. Reb Yechezkel acquired a permit from the police and climbed a perilous 50-rung ladder to retrieve the *get,* so that he would be able to fulfill his guarantee to the soldier.

A poor woman once came to Reb Yechezkel with a *shailah* about a chicken. Reb Yechezkel determined that the chicken was not kosher and took ten shillings out of his pocket, saying, "The chicken cannot be eaten — here is ten shillings." The woman refused the money until he raised his voice: "I am a Rav. I ruled that the chicken is *treif* and you accepted my ruling. I also rule that you must accept the money!"

ASIDE FROM his *Beis Din* activities, Reb Yechezkel gave countless *shiurim* for hundreds of people. His devotion to *emmes,* truth, would never permit him to veer from the topic or relate any anecdotes during a Talmudic discourse.

Once when he was invited to address a *siyum* with the traditional *hadran* — that is, connecting the conclusion of the Talmud with its beginning — Reb Yechezkel rose to speak and, to the chagrin of his audience, informed them that he would not say a *hadran* but rather clarify a certain halacha. When he saw their disappointment he related the following *Chazal:* "The Rabbis say that the Leviathan spans the entire breadth of the ocean so that his tail touches his mouth — thus connecting his beginning with his end. But, say *Chazal,* he is only playing, as it says, 'The Leviathan you have created to play with.' I, however, am searching for the truth and not to play!"*

On another occasion, while examining one of his *sefarim,* Reb Yechezkel sighed and said that each time he looked at this volume his heart ached. In it he quoted one of the *Gedolei Achronim,* who deduced the opposite of a well-known *Tosephos.* "I am certain that this *gadol* knew this *Tosephos,* but it probably slipped his mind for the moment. Did I really have to publicize that he temporarily forgot a *Tosephos?"*

The London *Beis Din* published several booklets based upon *shailos* that were asked of Reb Yechezkel, along with *Dinei Mamanos* and *Eretz Yisrael Nachlas Am Yisrael.* He also published several volumes of the *Tosephta* independently.

Reb Yechezkel personally gave generously to a number of causes — especially yeshivos. When a certain *gadol* described his yeshiva's financial crisis, Reb Yechezkel immediately approached a wealthy Jew and sought his support. The man agreed to donate the entire sum needed,

---

* Rabbi Abramsky gave a weekly class to students and *baalei battim* on the Torah portion. When they arrived at *Parshas Ki Saitzai,* he pondered how he would explain the topic of *Yif'as To'ar* (the beautiful woman captive the Torah allows one to marry) without generating a barrage of unbidden questions. As usual, he prayed to Hashem for inspiration and was blessed with an idea typical of the approach he often adopted: he started the class by saying, "The Torah descended to the very depths of man's knowledge, and permitted a trial of endurance that would be difficult to sustain; it is evident, however, that all other prohibitions underwent the same scrutiny and God determined that man can certainly stand up to them."

on condition that Reb Yechezkel would explain the words of the *Chazal,* "*Gadol hama'aseh min ha'oseh*" — he who petitions the doer is greater than the one who actually performs the deed.

"After all," said the rich man, "why should the Rabbi's reward be greater than mine? It is I who am donating the money!" Reb Yechezkel replied: "When I knocked on your door, I was so nervous I could hear my heart thump. You did not have to experience this fear... overcoming this trepidation is worth far more than the sum that you are donating."

IN 5711 (1951), when Reb Yechezkel made *aliyah,* the Torah giants of *Eretz Yisrael* gathered to greet him and many asked him to head their yeshivos. He chose to lecture at the Slabodka Yeshiva in Bnei Brak, which was under the leadership of Rabbi Yitzchak Isaac Sherr, the son-in-law of the "*Alter*" of Slabodka. For close to twenty-five years, he travelled from Jerusalem to Bnei Brak to deliver his famous *shiurim.* He used to say that he felt like a millionaire who owned two apartments, for he viewed the yeshiva in Bnei Brak as his second home.

The aim of his *shiurim* was to fulfill the commandment to teach Torah. Keeping this intention in mind while delivering the *shiur,* he said, was harder than both the preparation and the actual delivery of the *shiur.*

He provided his students with a *derech* — an approach to learning Talmud. He never understood the desire yeshiva students have to produce their own innovative and original interpretations. "When I am able to learn a page of *gemara* without any questions, I am a happy man," he said. "By contrast, when a yeshiva student doesn't find any questions, he is terribly disappointed."

Reb Yechezkel reviewed a passage of *gemara* eight times before he delved into the underpinnings of its meaning. He said that he would be embarrassed to ever appear before one of his teachers if he had forgotten one of their lessons: "They teach and I forget? Whatever they taught is guarded within me as if it were locked in a safe!"

In addition to excellence in learning, Reb Yechezkel taught his students *middos* — good character traits — and *emunah* — faith in God — in which he himself had achieved such excellence. In addition, Rabbi Abramsky also gave a weekly *shiur* for hundreds of residents of his Jerusalem neighborhood, Bayit Vegan.

AFTER THE Six Day War, a tourist in Bayit Vegan asked him to explain the miracles which occurred during the war. Reb Yechezkel replied with a quotation from Psalms: "As the mountains surround Jerusalem, so does the Lord surround his people." He pointed to the mountains in the distance and said, "Just as these are a physical reality, likewise, God's surrounding and protecting His nation now and forevermore is a reality. That was proven in this war..."

When his eldest son, Rabbi Moshe Abramsky, died (two years before his own death), Reb Yechezkel said the words of Psalm 119 about himself: "I have chosen the way of truth, Thy judgements have I laid before me." For the one who grasps the way of faith, everything is fair — God's attribute of justice is just like God's attribute of mercy.

At a time when it appeared that the army would draft yeshiva students, Shimon Peres, the Minister of Defense at the time, made an appointment with Reb Yechezkel, who was the head of the *Va'ad Hayeshivos,* and other *roshei yeshiva*. Rabbi Abramsky asked Mr. Peres for permission to begin with the very words with which he wished to conclude. Mr. Peres nodded his head. Rabbi Abramsky's face grew solemn as he said: "We wish to tell you that the subject is not a matter for discussion. The yeshivos are the home of life, and the Torah is the core of life, and one is not permitted to sever a life source!"

Mr. Peres turned over his briefing paper with his plan and suggestions as if to say, "I yield."

AT THE AGE of eighty-four, Reb Yechezkel suffered a heart attack and was not allowed to deliver any *shiurim*, a decree which pained him far more than the attack itself. After his recuperation, he was inspired to resume his *shiurim* by the visit of a student who demonstrated that he remembered Rabbi Abramsky's every word. The very next Shabbos the dining room of Yeshivas Kol Torah in Bayit Vegan was packed for the long-awaited *shiur*. When Reb Yechezkel arrived at the *gemara* which interprets Psalm 92 *Mizmor Shir Leyom HaShabbos*, he explained the entire chapter verse by verse:

"Planted in the house of the Lord, they shall flourish in the courts of our God." He pointed to an inconsistency in the grammar of the two words "planted" and "flourish," which occur in two different tenses. The explanation he suggested is that when a *tzaddik* leaves this world, he is already planted in the world-to-come; however, his influence here continues to increase after his death — thus flourishes, in the present tense — through his influence over the many who follow his path.

How appropriate are these words to Reb Yechezkel himself. On that *motzei* Shabbos, Elul 24, 5736 (1976), Reb Yechezkel Abramsky was invited to the Divine Court after serving God and His people through His Torah for over ninety years. His Torah teachings, however, continue to flourish.

In his great humility, he requested that in place of eulogies, it be announced at his funeral that he asks everyone for forgiveness and that he forgives everyone.

The Last Hundred Days

REB CHAIM SHMUELEVITZ *zt"l* (5663/1902-5739/1978) was the famed dean of the Mirrer Yeshiva in Jerusalem. Son-in-law of the previous Mirrer *Rosh Yeshiva,* Reb Eliezer Yehudah Finkel *zt"l,* he had already assumed a position of leadership during the yeshiva's exile in Shanghai in the World War II era. He succeeded his father-in-law in 1965, and was recognized as one of the world's greatest scholars and *roshei yeshiva.*

※

THOSE LAST hundred days... the heart aches at the remembrance. As a flame ascends just before it burns out, so were our hopes raised at the end only to be extinguished.

When Reb Chaim, the *Rosh Yeshiva,* failed to appear on Rosh Hashanah, it was evident how ill he was. His absence was pronounced for Reb Chaim's daily presence was so conspicuous that his nonappearance was as tangible as the sudden removal of all the *shtenders* (lecterns) from the yeshiva might have been. We did not know what his ailment was; his family would tell us only to learn and say *Tehillim* for him.

ON *KOL NIDRE* night the *Rosh Yeshiva* was helped into the *beis midrash*. In his later years, Reb Chaim had never looked too well. Although his smile at the news of a *chassan,* a birth, a *chiddush,* a *yeshua* (salvation) for *Klal Yisrael* etc., could light up a room, he looked every day of his age. But on that night he looked — Hashem *yerachem!*

After resting for but a few minutes he ascended the steps adjacent to the *aron kodesh* to address the yeshiva: "Yom Kippur cannot atone until one appeases his neighbor." His eyes welled with tears as he repeated himself. We did not know it at the time, but this was his last address; he was asking for forgiveness. As he feebly descended the stairs in obvious pain he stopped and exclaimed, *"Zeht vuss ken verren fun ah mentsch"* — "Look at me! Look what can become of a man." The most powerful Yom Kippur *drasha* (speech) ever uttered in just seven words.

THE NEXT MORNING Reb Chaim was confined to bed and could not come to *davening.* At the end of *Ne'ila* there was only one thought in our minds. When we reached *Avinu Malkeinu* at the conclusion of *Ne'ila* the yeshiva was ablaze with the fervor of our prayers.

Avinu Malkeinu, our Father, our King, remember us favorably, seal us in the book of happy life, *Avinu Malkenu!* Our Father, our King, *shlach refuah sheleimah lecholei amecha* — Send a complete recovery to the sick of your nation, especially to Chaim Leib ben Ettel! The windows vibrated; the walls seemed to shake; the *tefillah* was thunderous. In Heaven it was heard; he was living on borrowed time.

ON *HOSHANAH RABBA* a man knocked on the door of the Shmuelevitz apartment to ask the *Rosh*

Yeshiva to pray on behalf of a sick person. The family refused, for Reb Chaim was already critically ill. Over their protests, however, the visitor managed to enter and presented the *Rosh Yeshiva* with a slip of paper on which the sick person's name was written. Reb Chaim recognized the name and insisted that he be taken to the *Kosel* (Western Wall) to pray for the *choleh*. The family stared incredulously at Reb Chaim. They tried to dissuade him, but as they knew only too well, trying to oppose the dictates of Reb Chaim's heart was no facile endeavor.

The *Rosh Yeshiva* had always followed the dictates of his heart; his benevolent concern for his fellow Jew was legendary. Long before, he had shepherded the yeshiva exiles in Shanghai during the war, as he did later for both foreign and local students in Jerusalem. Every *erev* Yom Kippur he would go to *Kever Rochel* and weep. "Rochel our Mother, *Hakadosh Baruch Hu* requests you to hold back your tears. The Father wants you to stop crying, but your son Chaim Leib asks you to persist. Go before His throne of glory and beg mercy for your children living in oppression..."

Despite the family's adamant refusal, a taxi was ordered to convey Reb Chaim to the Old City. He had to be helped inside, and from the taxi was literally lifted to the *Kosel,* for he no longer had any strength of his own. He uttered a fervent prayer, was carried back to the car and was returned to his bed.

WE WERE NOT privileged to see Reb Chaim during Sukkos. We danced on *Simchas Torah* without the *Rosh Yeshiva,* our exemplar of Torah. But after the *hakafos,* Reb Chaim was helped into the *beis midrash*. The song changed to *"se'uh she'arim rosheichem"* and we moved aside as if we had rehearsed his entrance a dozen times.

Reb Aryeh Finkel, the *ba'al koreh* and *ba'al tefillah* (cantor), began to read the *R'shus LeChassan Torah*.

Meir'shus haKayl hagadol, hagibor, v'hanorah... hanosenes osher vechovod v'sipharah, God who provides happiness, honor, life and splendor... His eyes began to water and his throat started to swell. Each word was muffled in tears and sobs. The words of the traditional cantillation could no longer be distinguished.

Hama'areches yamim u'mosephes gevurah — Who adds days and increases strength — each word was dissolved in tears.

U'v'chein yehi ratzon milifnei haGevurah lasais chaim vachessed va'atarah le Rabi Chaim Leib ben Rephael... Therefore let it be the will before the Almighty to provide life, kindness and splendor to Rebbe Chaim Leib ben Rephael...

The entire yeshiva was on the brink of tears.

Amod, Amod, Amod, Arise, Arise, Arise, *moreinu v'rabbeinu,* our master and our teacher, *Rav Chaim Leib Chassan HaTorah.*

His son-in-law and some married students helped him rise to his feet. Both arms supported, he was led to the Torah. This was to be Reb Chaim's last *aliyah*. He uttered each word with agonizing pain. How fitting that the *masmid* who spent every waking hour engaged in Torah study, was to hold the *Sefer Torah* for the last time as her groom!

FROM THEN on Reb Chaim's condition deteriorated drastically. *Tehillim* were recited around the clock. "*Zechus* (merit) petitions" were circulated, hoping to express the vital need Reb Chaim filled. Dozens of married students promised to attend, upon recovery, the *va'adim* and *chaburos* (various classes and lectures) the *Rosh Yeshiva* offered. One sheet, hundreds of signatures long, was a declaration to learn an extra amount every day for the *zechus* of the *Rosh Yeshiva*.

On the last day of the yeshiva recess, the 29th of *Tishrei*, Reb Chaim was admitted to Shaarei Tzedek Hospital when his illness was aggravated by a severe case of pneumonia. The doctors predicted that he would not survive the weekend. A *mishmar* (all-night study session) was called that Thursday in the yeshiva. The yeshiva *bochurim,* joined by married students who remained in the yeshiva, learned with burning diligence all night long. At 11:30 p.m. the yeshiva was as crowded as it normally is in the midst of afternoon *seder* (session). At midnight, prayers were recited, immediately followed by the resumption of learning.

On Sunday, Monday and Tuesday a *minyan* worked in shifts around the clock, learning and reciting *Tehillim* for the *Rosh Yeshiva.* In the middle of the week doctors announced that to their astonishment the pneumonia had cleared up; nevertheless, the danger not yet over. The reports we received from the hospital were far from optimistic and the situation remained critical. A grandchild overheard Reb Chaim utter *viduy;* nurses reported no improvement.

On Thursday the yeshiva *davened* the *Yom Kippur kattan* service and the *Rosh Yeshiva*'s name was changed by Reb Aryeh Finkel to *Yosef* Chaim Leib. *Repha'einu* in *chazaras hashatz* seemed endless: each word was drowned in tears and barely audible.

"Yosef Chaim Leib ben Ettel" became the focus of our prayers. Countless times the yeshiva poured down *en masse* to the *Kosel* to pray on his behalf. Our prayers were echoed around the world: each yeshiva recited *Tehillim* with the same resolve. The Mirrer Yeshiva sponsored several *kinusei his'orrerus* (arousal assemblies) for the *Rosh Yeshiva*'s recovery. At each and every one the yeshiva was filled to capacity to hear leading Torah authorities awake us to prayer. The *Gedolei Hador* issued a proclamation for a universal day of prayer devoted to Reb Chaim.

Every spiritual avenue was pursued to restore the *Rosh Yeshiva*'s health. All were keenly aware of what was at stake; we sensed the dimension of the imminent tragedy. Reb Moshe Feinstein said on the telephone that "the world rested upon Reb Chaim's shoulders."

HIS NAME actually said it all: "Chaim Leib" — the living lion. He reigned in the Torah world as a lion in his domain — until his very last day.

A week before he passed away, a relative visiting him in the hospital wished him a speedy recovery. No longer able to discern what was being said to him, Reb Chaim responded, "*Breng ah rayah*" (present a proof), assuming, typically, that he was being addressed concerning a Torah thought.

Reb Chaim, however, was the one to "bring a proof." For years, the Rambam's *halacha* in the laws of Talmud Torah has been a source of perplexity. How could the Rambam require (1:8) "even one afflicted with pain to study Torah"? Those agonizing last months when the *Rosh Yeshiva*'s life hung by a thread, his fist yet moved in concentric circles, his mouth still uttered fragments of Torah, his brain was still active... Reb Chaim was the embodiment of a "proof" for the Rambam.

We held our breath. Reb Chaim used to say that prayer has the power to ward off death. We tried. We tried to hold on to a *gadol* from the previous generation, a man who had mastered Torah in its entirety in both depth and clarity. There should be words to express his greatness, but we lack them.

We could not hold on. We stormed the Gates of Heaven, but apparently we were undeserving. As the last of the Chanukah candles sputtered out on the evening of the third of *Teves, Klal Yisrael*'s glowing beacon also ceased to radiate.

THE FOLLOWING morning there was a funeral of unprecedented proportion in the annals of *Klal Yisrael*. Everyone seemed to be there, *chassidim, misnagdim,* from Torah giants to simple carpenters whose shops border the Mirrer Yeshiva. Almost a hundred thousand mourners stood outside the yeshiva under the brilliant December sun while eulogies were delivered. Local bus service was suspended; the police didn't even try to contain the crowds. After the last eulogy, a human chain began to uncoil, sprawling over the entire breadth of Jerusalem. Just as the tail of the procession was leaving the Mirrer Yeshiva, the head of the *levayah* (funeral procession) arrived at *Har HaMenuchos* (the cemetery). The religious neighborhoods were like ghost towns; every shop was closed and the streets deserted.

The *talmidim* began to trickle back to the yeshiva in the early evening. Glass panes in the halls had been smashed by the tremendous crush of the crowds. Our clothes were rent as is required for the passing of a close relative. The *paroches* (ark curtain) was returned to the *aron kodesh* (ark) and benches were slowly replaced in preparation for the eulogies which would take place during the next six nights.

Thousands came to console the Shmuelevitz family during the week of *shiva* (mourning). Previously unknown stories of the *Rosh Yeshiva*'s greatness began to circulate, tales so amazing that they were hard to believe but easy to inspire — things we cannot hope to achieve, but for which we can yearn and strive.

A PURIM PASSING

> *The Hebrew word for charity is justice, for Jews never separated charity from duty. The mitzva of charity is incumbent upon all Jews although some clearly conceived their obligation in extraordinary dimensions.*

J ERUSALEM — city of many charities, and the finest *gabboim* (collectors, treasurers). Not very long ago the city once had a major architect. He erected palaces out of *chessed*; skyscrapers out of *tzeddaka*. Reb Yosef Binyomin Rubin *zt'l*, was perhaps the greatest *gabbai tzeddaka* Jerusalem has ever known.

One cannot transcend overnight. His capacity for charity was partly indigenous, partly cultivated. The result was a paragon so exalted that he became a legend in his very own time.

From the time that he was a child he had an inner drive to give *tzeddaka* which would afford him no rest.

> Directly after his wedding, during the week of *sheva brachos*, adorned in a *shtreimel* and *bekashe* and accompanied by a *shomer* (guard), he stood on the street corner collecting *tzeddaka*.

"Do the poor people have to suffer just because I have a *simcha*?"

RABBI RUBIN revolutionized giving *tzeddaka* by introducing radical concepts in the art of giving. He contended that one must give according to the poor person's need and not according to the giver's means. He borrowed terms from the inflation-plagued Israeli economy to help the indigent: Poor people must also have wage increments, price increases, value added supplements etc., he reasoned.

To cover his budget he borrowed staggering sums of money from a free-loan society every month. He borrowed because he felt that he had a personal debt which had to be paid; he wasn't doing the poor a favor, he was merely carrying out an obligation. Rabbi Yosef Rubin assumed a quarter of the debts of many a new marriage, living up to his namesake: "*Yosef hu hamashbir...* is the provider."

Poor people are all the same. Sephardi, Ashkenazi, Chassid, Misnagid, whatever; all have the same needs of life's necessities and dignity. Rabbi Rubin's greatest joy, however, was to provide for a *talmid chacham*.

> *An impoverished talmid chacham did not even have a jacket to wear. Reb Yosef purchased a wardrobe for him, and could not help boasting: "I have just bought a cover for a Sefer Torah."*

He was an undercover detective of the highest order. No matter what the camouflage — Reb Yosef saw through it. He had an uncanny nose for detecting who was truly in need; and when he found a worthy recipient — nothing stood in his path. Some way or another the needy received, usually never realizing how, when, or from where.

> *One day he noticed that a member of his Kollel was extremely upset. Reb Yosef was convinced that this man's anger stemmed from a deficit of funds. Rabbi Rubin went home, gathered some money, and ended up rescuing this fellow's family life just in time.*

Providing for the needy, more than 300 families on a weekly basis, represented half a million pound* expenditure for *Pesach* alone!

HIS DAY commenced at four in the morning. He prayed at sunrise and then went collecting until nine o'clock when the second part of his day began. At nine o'clock he began to study Torah with all of the diligence of a person who was just beginning his day.

Every day he travelled to a different *shul* — Wednesday for example, was "Bayit Vegan day" — and he travelled at his own expense. Every *Lag B'Omer* he would journey to Meron, and stand for 14 hours on his feet collecting *tzeddaka*.

"*Yidden gibb tzeddaka*" was his motto; *bracha, hatzlacha vechol tuv,* his ancillary blessing. These familiar words always evoked a positive response. Everyone had so much faith in him that there was never a question of trust. On a hot day he used to buy a soda and say with a grin, "Let everyone's doubt of my veracity be invested in this drink."

JERUSALEMITES will never forget Purim 5737. It was a *Purim Meshulash* — three consecutive days of celebration, bedecked with snow. Early in the evening the snow began to fall. Late into the night it still hadn't stopped, and there was an eerie feeling that this was a sorrow-clouded harbinger.

Everyone in the Rubin house was still awake. Reb Yosef was ill, but threatened to go out the next day collecting for the poor nonetheless.

"But you're not well!"

---

* Years ago, when the pound (which preceded the shekel) was relatively stable.

"What?! It's Purim, the holiday of *aniyim* (the poor)!"
"No!" they insisted, "you are not allowed to leave your bed."

But as his family knew only too well, fighting Reb Yosef's heart, his concern for fellow Jews, was a Herculean task.

Early the next morning Reb Yosef was out celebrating Purim by collecting for the poor, trudging through the snow, battling his illness, and fighting the weather. The fatigue was apparent and his knees gave way.

Jerusalem's greatest *gabbai tzeddaka* lay motionless on the freezing asphalt. Reb Yosef was rushed to the hospital for emergency treatment to help him regain consciousness. But nothing seemed to work. Not a move, not a twitch.

His family gathered around his bedside day and night. Specialists from all over tried every possible method to return him to consciousness. Still nothing. Nothing until his wife went over to the bedside and whispered, "Yosel, it's time for *kimcha dePischa*."* His eyes opened and he began to cry.

Two weeks after Purim, Reb Yosef was buried. On his gravestone were engraved the words that he had willed:

גבאי צדקה שלא על מנת לקבל פרס

A Gabbai tzeddaka, without salary.

Jerusalem was in shock. Hundreds of sephardi women asked the family "*Aifo Yosef?*" They could not accept that he had died. "How can we make a *chag* (holiday) without

---

*Pesach help for the needy; customarily collections begin thirty days in advance of the holiday, the day after Purim.

him?" He died with a debt of IL250,000 ($25,000 at the time) to a free-loan society, but Jerusalem was bereaved with a far greater debt. The only consolation is that he is not dead in the hearts that he left behind; or put more succinctly, *od Yosef chai,* Yosef lives yet.

A Time to Mend

LAIL SHIMURIM

> *The Torah guarantees special protection to the Jewish people on the first night of Passover (Shmos 12:42), referred to as Lail Shimurim, the "night of watching." Destructive forces are not given reign on this night. Underground Muscovites have joined the long tradition of Jews willing to gamble on this protection.*

TRY AND OBSERVE Passover in Moscow. There aren't any matzos, kosher wine or meat; gathering together to celebrate a *seder* is all but illegal.

Recently, forty Jews decided to participate in a communal *seder* nonetheless. Each participant carefully thought over his decision. Was a one-night ceremony worth all of the inherent risks? Detection by the KGB (and who could avoid it?) was tantamount to arrest and incarceration. Parents would be guilty of religious indoctrination of Soviet youth (a felony) and university students would face immediate expulsion and automatic conscription into the army. Was a *seder* really necessary to impress upon a Soviet Jew the image of Egyptian subjugation?

Forty Moscow Jews did not view this question as hypothetical. Aside from the heroism called for, parents taught their children the ingenuity of Jewish enterprise. A clandestine *shmurah matzoh* bakery was set up and each fragile matzoh was smuggled out in a newspaper. As for the four cups, friends and relatives helped purchase the huge amounts of raisins needed for making the wine.

While this was going on, some of the participants looked over carefully prepared notes about how to conduct a *seder*. Cassettes of *Pesach nigunnim* circulated with joy and excitement among the friends.

Zev, the *seder* mastermind, suggested that since they had never attended a *seder* before they should conduct a rehearsal. Accordingly, Zev and Sasha secretly convened in Moshe's apartment in preparation for that momentous night. Using makeshift props: water substituting for wine, plates for matzos, a pen for the *zroa,* etc., the mock *seder* commenced.

IT WAS MORE than a week before *Pesach*, but for the three men sitting at the bare *seder* table, the excitement was already impossible to contain. By the time they reached *Hallel* in the Haggadah, they were hoarse from their hushed singing. But they couldn't stop. Each stanza about the slavery and the Exodus was so rich in meaning for them:

שומרים הפקד לעירך כל היום וכל הלילה
"Appoint watchmen to your city all day and all night"...

Bang, Bang, BANG!! It wasn't a knock at the door, but a thunder-clap intended to unsettle and frighten. The pounding was accompanied by the incessant ringing of the buzzer. The intruders weren't petitioning for permission to enter. Before they broke in they wanted to instill as much fear as possible. You never knew exactly what waited on the other side of the door. How many? How anti-Semitic? Had they brought along the hungry dogs who always managed to get loose for a few seconds...? Five men burst through the door and surrounded the three. They started shoving and shouting: "Jewish nationalist propaganda!" "Obstruction of socialist justice!" "Anti-Communist blasphemy!" "Zionist hooliganism!" etc. Each mouth parroted a different offense.

This went on for almost an hour, waking up all of the neighbors in the building. After examining the identity papers of the Jews, they threatened that one more violation of "anti-Soviet propaganda" would mean immediate arrest.

If the purpose of this raid was to frighten, it hardly succeeded. Of course, initially the three were scared and had trouble falling asleep, but they remained undaunted. Come what may, they were going to make a *seder*.

RIGHT BEFORE *erev Pesach*, the forty received permission to use someone's *dacha* (vacation home) at a relatively safer location, fifty kilometers southwest of Moscow. They made their exodus from the city one by one, each person carrying a portion of the precious *Pesach* cargo. The women worked like an experienced team to render the kitchen *kasher lePesach*, while the men helped out with the rest of the house. This little home had to double as a *shteible* and as a dormitory.

When evening arrived, the tired but jubilant men gathered in the dining room for *Maariv*. There were so many different types of Jews assembled in that *dacha*. For some it was their first *Maariv*, for others it was their first *Maariv* with a *minyan*. After they finished, they quickly took their seats around the special table. The air of expectation in that room was almost tangible. All eyes were turned toward Zev who started the *Kiddush*.

Afterwards, Moshe's son Chaim'ke asked the four *kashas*, "*Ma nishtana halaila hazeh mikol halailos?*" There wasn't a dry cheek in the room. *Ma nishtana halaila hazeh mikol halailos!* Why is this night different from all other nights?! On this night forty Jews chose to affirm their Judaism which they knew so little about. To stand up to a calculated campaign against such affiliation. On all other nights they can only *dream* about being a Jew and *leshana habaa beYerushalayim* (next year in Jerusalem). But tonight, tonight was so different! "We were once slaves to Pharaoh in Egypt. *'Maaseh avos siman lebanim* – the actions of fathers presage the events of the children' — how true it is. Laban tried to uproot everything — and he's still trying!"

The most attentive participant was dreamy-eyed Simon Eisikovitch. The last time he had attended a *seder* was fifty years ago, when he was just ten years old. For Simon, the thrill of the *seder* was mixed with cherished nostalgia — fifty years ago *he* had asked the *ma nishtana*. Simon remembered the sequence of the *seder* and offered instructions to the participants before Zev could read them out.

As THE *SEDER* continued, Zev's face suddenly turned pale. Looking up from the Haggadah he turned to Moshe and asked in a whisper, "Are we expecting anyone else?" Shadows outside the window began moving closer. Moshe, as calmly as he could, arose from the table and drew the shades tighter and double-locked the door. The responsibility resting on Zev's shoulders was awesome. He had not only invited all of the participants but had *convinced* them to attend. How could he bear the responsibility of causing parents and old people to be sent to Siberia? Zev lamely tried to assuage himself with the thought that it was *Lail Shimurim.*

But his conscience kept nagging at him, affording him no relief. The shadows were not disappearing. Simon, unaware of what was transpiring, announced that it was time to open the door for Elijah the Prophet. Zev tried to delay the continuation of the Haggadah, but Simon wouldn't hear of it. "Everyone rise for Elijah," Simon proudly announced. Zev told them that it was cold outside and opening the door wasn't really necessary. "Lately," he assured the group, "the custom of opening the door hasn't been observed..." Simon scoffed at the comment, accused

Zev of Reformism, and proceeded toward the door. Moshe intercepted him and stared at him for twenty long seconds until Simon finally took his seat.

IT WAS 2:00 in the morning and Zev was anxious to finish the *seder* — there was just so much you could rely on *Lail Shimurim*. Everyone wished each other, and promised themselves, the most fervent blessing of the evening: *"leshana habaa beYerushalayim."* All of the matzos and Haggadahs were quickly stashed away into various hiding places. Moshe peeked through the shade and found that the shadows had 'passed over.'

Parents of children and university students, potentially the greatest offenders in the eyes of the KGB, were recommended to leave the *dacha,* and to stay away until the following afternoon. At a quarter to seven in the morning the shadows reappeared, this time with their source in full evidence. Nine of them. They swarmed in like hawks and started searching the premises, not uttering a word. They found nothing, not a clue.

That night, an even more joyous second *seder* was conducted. Simon finally got to open the door for Elijah for it was *taka* — veritably — a *Lail Shimurim*.

RAISING HIS VOICE

> Overwhelmed by the financial difficulties thrust upon them from the moment they arrive on Western shores, most Russian Jews have little interest, let alone desire, to pursue the religious freedom finally available to them. And when the fulfillment of halacha conflicts with career opportunities the trial of faith becomes all the harder.

NAFTALI GINZBURG used to soar through the vast expanse of tone from *piano* to *forte* and back again in the Gorki Opera. He was part of a concert tour which took him to the major opera halls of Estonia, Lithuania and Moscow. And the audiences loved him.

Ginzburg commanded a fabulously even scale, with a rich, full-bodied lower and middle voice rare in lyric tenors. After every performance he was showered with flowers from the audience. But those days are long gone.

The shouts of "bravo" from Soviet audiences have been replaced by calls of *"Yasher Koach"* from Jerusalem worshippers. For Ginzburg is now a yeshiva student and is training to be a *chazzan* (cantor) — a development he could never have anticipated.

Ginzburg always viewed opera as a vaguely unkosher profession, but his voice was a gift that he could not ignore. He attended a music conservatory in Tashkent for five years and received an *MA* in orchestra conducting.

IF YOU ASK Ginzburg why he decided to become religious, he will fumble for an answer. He did not have a Jewish upbringing, and his parents, who had received a relatively Jewish education fifty years ago, have long since submerged their heritage into the Russian reality. Nonetheless, for some inexplicable reason, Ginzburg was curious about his Judaism.

His first chance to investigate his religious roots came when he emigrated to the U.S. Russians he met in New York recommended that he contact Rabbi Velvel Pearl, who was active in outreach programs for Soviet immigrants.

Ginzburg went to Rabbi Pearl and poured out his heart: he did tedious jewelry work all day long just to cover expenses, leaving him neither time nor energy to pursue Torah studies. Furthermore, he wanted to continue with his singing career.

THE IDEA of becoming a *chazzan* crossed Rabbi Pearl's mind, but he might just as well have suggested that Ginzburg become a surgeon. A good voice is indispensable to a *chazzan*, but so is familiarity with Jewish law.

Meanwhile, Ginzburg had himself begun thinking about becoming a *chazzan*. The solution he reached to overcome his ignorance of Jewish liturgy wasn't original, but it reflected a pragmatic approach: a week after meeting with Rabbi Pearl, Ginzburg auditioned before the dean of the cantorial program of the Reform movement's Hebrew Union College. The dean was ecstatic over Ginzburg's voice, and quickly dismissed Ginzburg's concern about his liturgical illiteracy.

But this was exactly what Ginzburg did not want to hear. He was, in fact, searching for religious commitment, even if it entailed inconveniences rather than accommodation. His brief flirtation with Reform, he confesses today, was motivated solely by mercenary considerations — "a sin" that he immediately regretted.

RABBI PEARL brought Ginzburg's problem to the attention of Chaim Rabinowitz, a simple man imbued with a lofty soul. When he hears about a Jew, especially one from Russia, looking for religious direction, or even just companionship, his door immediately flies open.

The Rabinowitz family and Ginzburg were an ideal match. The children loved him, and despite the sharp contrast of surroundings Ginzburg encountered, he quickly felt at home. He also began to feel very Jewish, for the Rabinowitzes are devout Jews whose joyous observance is infectious.

It also hurt Rabinowitz to see highly trained talent go to waste. He expressed the frustration caused by Ginzburg's idle voice to Yehuda Gordon, a talent scout for Jerusalem's Shvut Ami yeshiva, which caters for Jews from the Soviet Union.

Gordon listened carefully to Ginzburg's dilemma and was able to sympathize with his plight, not just as a *landsman* but as one who underwent a similar ordeal. Gordon was a popular movie producer in Russia, and after two painfully unsuccessful years of trying to continue his career in America he realized that he was no closer to Hollywood in New York than he had been in Moscow.

GORDON WAS OPTIMISTIC that Shvut Ami could help, and that evening he phoned Jerusalem to ask if there was a future for a young would-be *chazzan* who was just learning the *aleph-bais*. The reply, which came two days later, was mildly encouraging. It wasn't going to be easy, but it was worth a try.

And so, Naftali Ginzburg arrived in Israel. He was well

received by the Shvut Ami Yeshiva, which arranged lessons for him with *chazzan* Chaim Pollack, who had once been one of the most celebrated cantors in Jerusalem, if not the world. Pollack had lost his voice several years earlier and has since devoted himself to passing on the tradition of high-calibre *chazzanus* to an elite corps of his students.

Six years is the normal period of apprenticeship, but Ginzburg's conservatory training automatically eliminated four years from the course. Indeed, in less than one year, he had mastered "*Kabbolas Shabbos.*" He celebrated the service's completion with his debut at the podium of Shvut Ami.

PASSION is the very lifeblood of *chazzanus,* and Ginzburg demonstrated on that Friday night just how well equipped he is in that regard. His exquisite coloration and mighty crescendos resounded off "Kikar Shabbos" two blocks away like a great bronze bell. His delivery of *Lecha Dodi* swept the worshippers up in a flight of prayer and stentorian flair. As soon as he finished the service he was pelted by a barrage of *shkoachs*. It was then that Ginzburg, who had previously been timid and ashamed of his lack of knowledge, knew that he would attain his goal.

News of his virtuosity spread quickly throughout the city. A few weeks later, he was invited to lead the Sabbath eve service at the Ohel Rivka Synagogue, which is attended by Jerusalem's Chief Rabbi. Ginzburg had the worshippers in a thrall with the opening melody. People swore that they had not heard such *tefilla* — prayer — since the great Moshe Koussevitzky and Yossele Rosenblatt.

Naftali Ginzburg is not just a powerful singer. He is a former "refusednik," a newly observant Jew, and a fledgling *chazzan* in the grand Ashkenazi tradition. In a number of ways he embodies the dream of thousands of Soviet Jews to "make it" in accordance with their tradition in Eretz Yisrael.

THE DAY OF THE DONKEY

> The Torah ordains that every first born male donkey must be redeemed or have its neck broken (Shmos 13:13). The mitzva is still observed today as a reminder that God slew the Egyptian first-born males, both man and beast and redeemed the Jews from Egypt with a mighty hand.

SOME ASSOCIATE donkeys with hauling coal, towing canal boats, and plowing cotton fields. A few relate donkeys with the primordial one which Bilaam rode, and *Moshiach* will ride. But who associates them with their special mitzva — *Pidyon Petter Chamor*?

A recent invitation embossed in gold, placed in select Jerusalem locations, generated new associations for over 5,000 people.

> **BEROV AM HADRAS MELECH**
> In the midst of multitudes
> is a king glorified
> We are happy to announce
> that please God
> Tuesday, Parshas Bahaaloscha,
> 10 Sivan, 5742 a
> **PIDYON PETTER CHAMOR**
> will take place...

Pidyon Petter Chamor? The name rings a vague

memory like a vestige from a Temple service. Not exactly. It is actually a mitzva which is neither esoteric or mystical.

The Torah ordains that every first-born male ass must be redeemed with a lamb, to remember the slain Egyptian first-born. Asses not redeemed must be killed, teaching that withholding that which one mistakenly deems to be his own, is in fact sentencing it to destruction (S.R. Hirsch).

Despite the sublimity of this mitzva, the rarity of "Jewish" donkeys, the infrequency of surviving first-born males, and the cost involved (there are halachic loopholes to avoid the expense) means that it is rarely observed. When this mitzva was finally performed, however, it was an event second only in proportion to *Birkas Hachamah* in its mass participation. Bus drivers in a 10-block radius were incredulous: It wasn't a funeral or a *hafganna* (demonstration)... they didn't know what to make of the crowds. "Did *Moshiach* arrive?" a bus driver asked, staring at the thousands streaming through the streets.

BEIS ZUPNICK, the plaza adjacent to *Yeshivat Ahavat Shalom* where the *pidyon* (redemption) took place, turned into a human "Black Sea." Not since the enormous anti-stadium protest years ago has *Battei Varshaw* seen nearly as many people.

The center of attention were the distinguished *dayanim*, *rabbonim* and *roshei yeshiva* seated on the porch in front of *Yeshivat Ahavat Shalom*. Dozens of loudspeakers were strung across the plaza to project the forthcoming speeches on *inyannei deyoma* (the topic of the day).

Irrespective of the great rabbis sitting on the balcony, the likes of which are rarely gathered under one awning, the crowds strained and craned to see the hero of the day. Youngsters performed acrobatic feats — to try and land on the roof of *Ahavat Shalom* and get a better view.

BUT THE HERO was not to be found. A donkey, even a baby one, cannot be easily concealed. Where could he be? Rumor had it that he had stubbornly refused to ascend the stairs to the Yeshiva...

Finally from the direction of the street came an uproar of applause. Sephardi women started ululating at the top of their voices. CLAP, CLAP, CLAP — tens, hundreds, thousands began to clap to a beat.

A *moshavnik* bearing a donkey on his head (instead of the customary *kova tembel*) marched toward the Yeshiva. People parted before him in waves to let him through, and then re-squished to catch another glimpse. The donkey was raised onto a table to satisfy the curious crowd. Each of his ears was adorned with pearl and jewel necklaces, and garlands of flowers were looped around his neck. After a few minutes, he was joined by his counterpart, the lamb, to thunderous applause.

Then the *rabbonim* began their speeches while the audience fidgeted, in anticipation of the actual redemption service. *HeChacham* Hillel, owner of the *bechor*, explained the plain and mystical significance of this mitzva.

"Every mitzva corresponds to a part of the body and each mitzva is a *tikun* (mending) to the soul and all of *Klal Yisrael*... Since every Jew cannot perform each mitzva, the fortunate few who have the opportunity should keep their fellow Jews in mind...". The *Toldos Aaron Rebbe*, the *kohein* who accepted the *pidyon,* echoed this theme.

"This mitzva did not come easily," declared *Chacham* Hillel. "I have tried to perform it for eight years! There were miscarriages, first-born females, etc... until this *bechor* was born on Shavuos night!"

One speech followed another until... silence, total silence fell upon the area. You could hear traffic on *Rechov Yaffo*, four blocks away. *Chacham* Hillel raised the donkey with both hands while the *Toldos Aaron Rebbe* appointed a *shaliach* (agent) to raise the redeeming lamb for him... A heavy *Sephardi havarah* (accent) amplified over the P.A.:

> *BARUCH ATTA...*
> Blessed are you *Hashem,*
> King of the Universe...
> *Asher Kiddishanu...*
> Who has commanded us
> *Al pidyon...*
> To redeem our
> first-born he-asses.

AMEN, responded the audience, in an emotional pitch. A blessing was made on a new fruit followed by a "*Shehechiyanu.*" People smiled at each other and shook hands beaming at having witnessed a once in a lifetime mitzva. What do you wish someone at an occasion like this? *Nachas? Mazel Tov? Kein Yirbu?*

The audience was baffled for lack of a blessing, but nonetheless felt very blessed at having participated. Eventually they hit upon the appropriate greeting: *"Tizku lemitzvos."* May you be worthy of many more mitzvos!"

A KESUBA FOR OUR ANNIVERSARY

Four months after Lester and Rena Weisses' 31st wedding anniversary, they both remarried – each other. It was a brief and reverential ceremony; there wasn't a band, photographer, flowers or even bentchers. In fact, it wasn't even "an intimate family gathering"– but a kosher marriage it was.

ONE FRIDAY evening over thirty years ago, Lester Weiss met Rena Sheinberger at the Seitenstettengasse Synagogue in Vienna. At the time, Lester was working for the American Military Intelligence Service (MIS) headquartered in Vienna. Although his clandestine missions often brought him into the Russian occupation zone, he tried to return to the American sector to attend Shabbos services every week.

Following Rena Sheinberger's graduation from nursing school in 1944 she volunteered for the W.A.C.S. After the war, she was also stationed in Vienna, where she used to attend synagogue every Friday evening. It seemed like a *"glick shidduch"* — both United States Army officers who "just happened" to be in the same synagogue one Friday evening, thousands of miles away from home. And indeed it was. Not much later, Lester and Rena were *"chassan* and *kallah,"* (bride and groom) and were on their way back home to the States to be wed.

The wedding was strictly a family affair held in the

Sheinberger backyard, in Harrington Park, New Jersey. Lester requested that a rabbi preside, so Mr. Sheinberger arranged for Reverend Cohn, a *chazzan* from nearby Newark, to officiate. And they lived happily ever after... almost.

IN THE early sixties, a metamorphosis began to occur in the Weiss household. Lester, the more observant member of the family, began to intensify his commitment to Judaism and David, their eldest son, was sent to a Day School.

Through the years, the Weisses became true *baalei teshuva*. Lester, or Levi, began attending a local *shiur* (talmud class) and Rena entered the fold. Following Day School, David attended Yeshiva High School in New York and continued from there to Beis Midrash Govoha in Lakewood, New Jersey. After four years in Lakewood David married a charming girl from Flatbush, New York to the heartfelt delight of his parents.

Throughout the wedding celebration and during the following week of *sheva brachos,* Levi began to wonder about his own wedding: How kosher were his *eidim* (marriage witnesses)? [Jewish law provides that to be a witness, one's way of life must be in accord with the law]. Was his *kesuba* (marriage contract) satisfactory? [As a protective measure for Jewish women, a man and wife may not live together without a *kesuba,* which binds him to fulfill all marital obligations to her].

For years, David had been haunted by the same fear, but what was he to do? He could hardly tell his parents that he suspected their marriage ceremony to have been invalid, for that would be tantamount to saying that they had lived together without *halachic* sanction all these years! How could a son say this to his parents? He once thought of "misplacing" their *kesuba* to necessitate the drawing up of a new one, and then take care of other corrective measures at the same time. To his chagrin, however, he discovered that his mother kept her *kesuba* in a safe deposit box in the bank, rendering it inaccessible. His father's newly expressed concern gave David an opportunity to investigate the matter.

WITH HIS parents' consent, David called up his high school *rebbe,* Rabbi Mendel Frankel, who was friendly with the family and was well versed in Jewish law. Rabbi Frankel listened carefully to Mr. Weiss' recounting of exactly what transpired at the marriage ceremony 31 years ago, asked several questions, and promised to call back that evening, after he had researched the relevant laws. Three hours later, Reb Mendel called back and said, "This is a complex *sheilah* of rare sensitivity, and requires a *shei'las chacham* (query of an expert). You must find out if the witnesses who signed the *kesuba* were Torah-observant Jews, were they related in any way to your mother, your father, or to each other? Were there any Sabbath observing men present at the wedding ceremony?"

David researched the event carefully and reported back in detail: "One witness, who is not religious, is my mother's uncle. The other witness is *shomer Shabbos* (Sabbath observant), however, he is my father's uncle. My father told me that Reverend Cohn, the local *Kol Bo* (religious functionary) who officiated is an observant Jew. He had studied in a yeshiva in his native Hungary, sends his children to yeshiva and advocates mitzva observance. Aside from him and my great-uncle, there weren't any Sabbath observers present. My mother's father's name is Chaim Mendel. Menachem Mendel was entered in the *kesuba* by mistake; 'Rena' is also misspelled. I am not sure whether the text of the *kesuba* is correct, for I checked it against mine and there are differences."

Rabbi Frankel explained that quite aside from the fundamental question of whether their marriage was ever kosher, their *kesuba* is patently invalid, for lack of the two required witnesses. If the marriage is kosher, then they need merely draw up a new *kesuba*; if it was not, a new marriage ceremony is in order — preferably entailing a *minyan* (quorum of ten men), a *chupa* (marriage canopy), *yichud* (the couple alone in a private room); and, of course, acceptable witnesses and a ring.

UPON RABBI Frankel's suggestion, David consulted a renowned *poseik* (halachic authority) to determine his parents' marital status. David was asked to describe particulars about Reverend Cohn's level of observance and beliefs, and the exact relationship of his father's uncle — the only other religious Jew present at the wedding. The *poseik*, relying upon a lenient opinion, ascertained that two "kosher" Jews had witnessed the wedding: "Even though one of them was not specified as a witness, his very presence at the *chupa* allows him to serve in this capacity. So, Reverend Cohn qualifies. And since your father's relative is, as so you say, a maternal uncle, according to the Rambam's opinion he is also not disqualified. Together, these two witnesses legitimized your parents' marriage. A new *kesuba,* however, must be written up at once. I recommend that after the *kesuba* is filled out, your father give a plain ring belonging exclusively to him to your mother and say the marriage formula '*Harey at mekudeshes*... Behold you are consecrated to me with this ring in accordance with the law of Moses and Israel,' to avoid any doubts."

David told his parents that their marriage was fortunately kosher enough to preclude the need for a remarriage (*chupa, minyan, yichud, sheva brachos* etc.). However, a new *kesuba* must be drawn up and a new ring should be given. David called up Rabbi Frankel and relayed the instructions that he had received, adding that he and his parents could come over in an hour to take care of the *kesuba* and marriage.

By the time the Weisses arrived, Rabbi Frankel had already purchased a *kesuba de'erchasa* (the special kind of a *kesuba* used to replace a lost one). He was busy examining the text with a colleague, who later joined Rabbi Frankel as a witness for the *kesuba* and brief wedding ceremony.

Everything seemed in order; the names were filled in and the date and location affixed. After one more perusal, Reb Mendel and his colleague signed the *kesuba*. He then asked Mr. Weiss if the ring was his — "affirmative." "Then you may marry your *kallah*," he said with a smile.

"*Harey at mekudeshes lee betaba'as zu kedas Moshe veYisrael*" — the words every *chassan* declares to his *kallah*, affirming the holiness of Jewish matrimony, and the authority of the Rabbis in the realm of marriage. *Mazel Tov! Mazel Tov!* Rena, holding her *kesuba* examined her new ring while Rabbi Frankel warmly embraced Mr. Weiss... .

OUR RABBIS have elaborated upon the sanctity and eminent significance of marriage: A groom is compared to a king, a bride to a queen; their coronation takes place under the *chupa* upon which the Divine Presence rests. If the bride and groom are meritorious, celestial angels descend to celebrate with them; and upon hearing the seven benedictions, they answer: "*Amen!* May it be the Almighty's will!"

This "*Amen*" is never too late in coming.

MIGHTY MEN OF VALOR

> *Every seven years through the mitzva of shmittah* the residents of Eretz Yisrael testify that God is the creator of the world and owner of the land. No mitzva highlights this realization more than shmittah, for normally one performs a mitzva for one day, or a week, but this mitzva lasts an entire year! One sees his fields and trees open to all, his fences unlocked, his fruit being eaten... and overcomes his natural instincts and does not object. People possessing such power of restraint are referred to as "mighty men of valor who perform His bidding." (Midrash Rabba).*

FAR MORE than just closing up shop for a year, the mitzva of *shviis* (seventh year) calls for relinquishing the feeling of being a *baal habayis* — proprietor of the land. Vanquishing the desire to be an exclusive owner is so difficult that the Torah testifies "there is no hero mightier than he."

The heroism of *shmittah* has a piquant history — be it a crucial battle that the Maccabees won because the enemy lost morale when the food they had hoped to plunder was depleted because of *shmittah* observance (*Toldos Yisrael,* Yavetz Vol 4, pp. 102-3), or the taxes from which Alexander the Great and Julius Caesar absolved the Jews on the seventh year. But the most stimulating *shmittah* in recent history was that of 5726 (1965-6), the year of the great potato and molasses crisis.

SIX WEEKS prior to Rosh Hashanah (when the *shmittah* year commences) forms were posted for *shviis* observers to register, to aid in calculating the needs of the observing community. Apparently this only affected a minor measure of relief, for a kilo of *shviis* kosher fruit was difficult to find in Jerusalem. At that time Arabs provided 20% of the fruit and vegetable supply, but this was either commingled with Jewish produce (non-kosher *leshviis*) or was snatched by the nearby rural *shmittah* observers.

The only resort was to isolate this 20% and providently channel it to specially designated stores and stations. This proved rather difficult, for Arab dealers tended to surreptitiously include less-expensive Jewish fruits and vegetables in their costly "*shviis*-free" produce. Another headache was trying to battle the Israel Chief Rabbinate's widely accepted *heter mechirah* — dispensation allowing Jews to work the ground based on a dubious loophole of selling the upper crust of the Land of Israel to a Gentile. The natural hardships and unbrotherly taunts which accompany *shmittah* observance after the Rabbinate declared *shviis* academic requires unusual faith and fortitude. It was this kind of fortitude that was put to the test in 5726.

POTATO is the staple of the Israeli Passover; ingredients commonly accepted abroad have never met local sanction. In early '66 thousands of tons of *kosher leshviis* potatoes were stored for the upcoming Passover. When this supply ran out well before the holiday, panic struck the *shmittah* observers. Whereas the religious consumer had come to live with the higher prices, inferior quality and small variety *shmittah* brought with it; the prospect of not having potatoes on Passover meant virtual starvation. Israeli Arabs who provide the bulk of the *kosher leshviis* produce do not grow potatoes.

Members of the *Badat'z vaad hashmittah (shmittah committee)*, who had launched a campaign and had exerted significant pressure on people to commit themselves to observe *shviis* and had guaranteed their constituents the Divine promise: "I will command my blessing upon you in the sixth year, and it shall bring forth fruit for three years" (*Vayikra* 25:21), were under swelling communal pressure. Threats and anonymous messages visited their homes and office with frequent succession.

WITH DELIBERATE speed the *vaad* members tried to cross the paper curtain of Israeli bureaucracy to attain an import license for more than 1,000 tons of potatoes, which was eventually forthcoming. (Simultaneously attempts were made to acquire an import license for grapes for kosher *leshviis* wineries. The powerful lobbies of the non-*shviis* wineries ensured that their monopoly wasn't cracked).

The *vaad* immediately contacted Cypriote dealers, the closest accessible potato farmers to Israel, in the hope of landing a deal for the desired amount. They quickly arranged a transaction and quiet and cheer were restored to Jerusalem and Bnei Brak. Once again the members of the *vaad hashmittah* were able to roam the streets without fear of attack or verbal violence... That is until just a few weeks before Passover when Israel received word that the order was sidetracked due to "increased Egyptian potato consumption."

When news of this fiasco hit town, members of the *vaad* could not be found. Ostensibly, they were out looking for potatoes, but health reasons also mandated their absence from Jerusalem. In point of fact, the members of the committee ended up in Nicosia scouring the countryside for any overstocked potato farms. Their arrival in Cyprus was quite a sight. Fair-skinned gentlemen with long white beards, *payos*, long black coats and oval hats contrasted quite noticeably with the local garb. They were also a bit hard-pressed in finding a local farmer conversant in Yiddish. Eventually, however, the *vaad shomrei shmittah* stumbled upon a Cypriote dealer who was willing to respond to Israeli pleas with several tons of over-priced potatoes.

MISSION ACCOMPLISHED, the *vaad* sailed for home relieved that they had averted a major crisis. Once again it was the *shmittah* committee to the rescue and acute resourcefulness which saved the day. That Shabbos, the one preceding *Shabbos Hagadol*, the *shmittah* agents received a hero's welcome at their respective congregations. That *motzei Shabbos* they received vexatious tidings over the phone. Cyprus was on the line confirming that the deal was secure but the boat wouldn't dock in Haifa until *erev Shabbos Hagadol,* (two days before *Pesach* which started on *motzei Shabbos*). This meant that the potatoes would remain in their seaside sacks until the completion of the holiday.

The receiver was barely replaced and the *vaad* was once again dialing dozens of inter-Mediterranean phone calls. There was only one solution left — a direct sea route to shorten the trip. The *shmittah* committee mustered its navigational and maritime prowess and at last such a route (Famagosta-Lymasol) was hit upon. The cost of the shipping was much higher but at least the valuable cargo would reach Israel in time.

Representatives of the *vaad* heavily laden with *baksheesh* were dispatched to Haifa to see to it that this boat would get the most expedient treatment when it arrived and that crews would be on hand to quickly unload the goods onto awaiting trucks. While all this was going on a rumor circulated that the ship had been hauled into Sardinia for repair. The rumor, thank God, turned out to be false and the boat arrived just in time.

The Haifaite longshoremen, notorious for their *moñana modus operandi,* worked with genuine alacrity, even foregoing their daily siesta, guaranteeing the boat's unloading before nightfall. Early the next morning breathless Jerusalemites, Bnei Brakers, Kommemius residents and other *shmittah* observers received their rationed potatoes with obvious relief and gratitude to *Hashem.*

An EVEN greater problem arose that same *shmittah* when one of the country's two yeast factories, which had served the *shviis* observers in previous years, closed down. This left Israel with only one yeast producer — yeast being a necessary ingredient in all breads. The remaining factory manufactured yeast from domestic ingredients which are not kosher *leshviis.* From the moment the yeast plant closed the committees of all the *shmittah* observing circles joined hands to push for a radical enterprise. It was inconceivable that the one and only factory in the state could produce both kosher and non-kosher *leshviis* yeast; the koshering procedure alone between productions would entail days if not weeks of hard, expensive labor.

Representatives of the various committees entered fatiguing negotiations with the active factory and the Ministry of Commerce and Industry to import a quantity of molasses, one of yeast's major ingredients, for all the residents of Israel. All of these negotiations were held in the backdrop of the Israel Chief Rabbinate's *heter* — sale of the land to non-Jews, stiff lobbying from the domestic molasses producer and a serious deficit in the national balance of payments. If word of these negotiations had been leaked to Israel's rabid anti-religious press, a scandal of "ultra-Orthodox anti-Zionist extortion" would have inevitably ensued, jinxing the deal from the outset.

THE *VAAD HASHMITTAH* requested the Jerusalemites to "pray for bread." Potato fever was in the air again, this time for *chometz*. On the evening that the factory had used its last drop of pre-*shmittah* produced molasses, Israel's prayers were acknowledged with a go-ahead for the deal.

Once again thanks was given for the cooperation of all the involved parties and their brilliant diplomacy; and credit awarded to the inspiring inactivity of those who keep the laws by giving the sacred soil its rest.

SOMETHING NEW UNDER THE SUN

> *Every twenty eight years the sun returns to the precise location in the sky where God placed it on the fourth day of creation more than 5700 years ago.* **Such a rare event cannot just roll around unnoticed. To mark this occasion there is a special blessing which praises the Lord who "performs the act of creation... oseh maaseh Bereishis."*

THERE IS something about Jerusalemites that love a spectacle. The principle *Berov Am Hadras Melech*, "In the midst of multitudes is a king glorified" takes on especial

---

* The date of the blessing is calculated by dividing the solar year into weeks, which yields fifty-two weeks (364 days), with one day and six hours remaining. The differential between one solar year (*tekufah*) and the next is thirty hours. The cumulative differential after four years equals 120 hours (30 x 4), which is equivalent to five complete days. On the fifth year the *tekufah* commences on the very same hour as the original *tekufah* four years earlier; this is called *machzor kotton* (Meiri on Brachos 59b).

   Although every fifth year starts on the same hour as the original *tekufah*, it does not come out on the same day as the first year of the *machzor kotton*. The *tekufos* finally return to the same hour and day of the week as they started, i.e., were created, when the yearly differential of 30 hours add up to an even week, i.e., 840 hours, which equal 35 days — five complete weeks. This aggregate is achieved every 28 years and is called *machzor gadol*. The exact date of the blessing varies from cycle to cycle.

** The stars were placed in the firmament in the evening of the fourth day

meaning in the Holy City. And when the sight is a *dvar mitzva*, there is simply no way of containing the crowds.

It was still dark and overcast on 4, Nissan 5741 (1981), but the streets of Jerusalem were streaming. The volume of traffic and pedestrians far exceeded peak rush hour. Although there were several sites where communal *Birkas Hachamah*s were held, everyone seemed to be headed to the *Kosel* (Western Wall).

As each of the hundreds of buses dispatched to service the event pulled up to an overcrowded bus stop they were filled instantaneously to double their capacity. The flow of human seas rushing towards the Old City barely made room for the surge of traffic headed in the same direction.

One could perceive the miracle of *aliyas regel* — the holiday-pilgrimages in the time of the Temple. A crowd of 120,000 crammed every rooftop and courtyard in Jerusalem's Old City.

The massive *Birkas Kohanim*, clearly 2,000 strong, gave a glimpse of the miracle of עומדים צפופים ומשתחוים רוחים — "Though the people stood closely pressed together, they found ample space to prostrate." (*Avos* 5:7) The communal prayer itself was an unforgettable event, but the milestone was still to come.

AFTER THE completion of *Shacharis,* the P.A. informed everyone to slowly move away from the *Kosel* in order to see the sun's rising. "Slowly," repeated the announcer, "the slightest push could be disastrous, God forbid!" After the giant shift everything was ready and set — except the sun. The overcast sky began to darken. Although probably few

---

of creation. The sun, however, did not shine until twelve hours later, that is, Wednesday morning (*Chazon Ish* 138:7) and this is when the benediction is made.

out of the thousands had actually waited 28 years just for this event, certainly most of them had waited weeks if not months in anticipation of this special day — and it started to rain... It was as if God was showing His displeasure and saying "I'm not going anywhere — I'll be here 28 years from now — but it is up to you to mend your ways and solve your differences..."

The P.A. then boomed out for everyone to join in the recitation of *Tehillim*. 120,000 voices rose in unison. It was prayer so powerful that it could alter the weather — and it did. Clouds began to recede and the *Tehillim* roared louder. One cloud after another rolled away to the north and the *Tehillim* didn't stop. The first rays of the sun began to crack through... Just one thin cloud still covered the sun and was beginning to head in the direction of the others. The person who was leading the *Tehillim* tapered off, and everyone thumbed in their *siddurim* or special pamphlets for the *bracha* and accompanying verses that were to be said.

Heads jockeyed back and forth between the sky and the plaza on top of the steps which descend to the *Kosel* where the *Poskim* were standing. The order to recite the blessing would come from the plaza. And then... there it was, a big yellow ball in all of its glory.

BORUCH ATTAH HASHEM... OSEH MAASEH BEREISHIS.

The emotion that had been simmering came to a head. Whoever had problems of faith cleared them away — the *Tehillim* had literally vanquished the weather. The same sun seen every day suddenly became so special; a feeling of such appreciation and gratitude swept the crowd. A boys' choir took over the P.A. and struck up a special tune composed for the occasion. Everyone wished each other, perfect strangers, a good year, a good life — we'll meet again, please God, in 28 years!

THE CROWD started swarming out of the Old City towards *Rechov* Yaffo. The band led the way while everyone marched behind. Arabs who were just arriving for work from the territories and Bethlehem stood back in awe. The throng coming out of Jaffa Gate just didn't end. Fear gripped the Arabs and they started jumping into buses and running down the valley.

In the meantime the crowd marched on like a ticker tape parade. Where were they headed? No one knew — no one cared. Arms locked and spontaneous circles of dancers started spinning off like space ships. Soldiers and *chassidim, misnagdim,* and simple bystanders all joined the circles.

The procession headed up through Geula until "Kikar Shabbos" where it met up with the crowd that had blessed the sun in "Battei Hungarin." *Chassidishe, Yerushalimer* women with black *tichels* pulled tightly over their heads stood on the sides, their faces flushed with tears. Who could hold back their emotions? Where were they twenty-eight years ago? Look at what has transpired. Who knows where they will be — or what will be 28 years hence?

There was something new under the sun.

HOSPITALITY IS HOMEMADE

"Hospitality is greater than greeting God Himself" (Talmud). Little wonder that those who perform this mitzva do so with such alacrity and zeal. Throughout the ages, Jews in communities the world over have never hesitated to make a perfect stranger feel at home. It is wise to remember, however, that hospitality begins with the invitation.

HOSPITALITY is one of those mitzvos that we love to hear tales about more than perform. Maybe the stories sound too apocryphal; and they just titillate rather than inspire. After all, *Eliyahu Hanavi* isn't disguised anymore as a poor man roaming the streets looking for a tenderhearted family; and even if he is out there, he certainly isn't Jeff from Hartford or Catherine from Johannesburg.

There was a time when not only *Eliyahu Hanavi* was a sought after guest. Anyone who needed a place or a meal was more than welcome. Of course, being hospitable in the past had its fringe benefits... Guests were reputed to have turned diluted grape juice into expensive old wine and perform a host of other miracles. Today they merely help with the dishes and tell their life stories.

In any event, if the guests have changed the mitzva hasn't — it is still greater than greeting the Divine Presence. And gradually people are beginning to learn this...

A Time to Keep

ONE FRIDAY AFTERNOON a *yungerman* in Mattersdorf, Jerusalem received a frantic phone call to accept a guest who was "just picked up at the Western Wall." The telephone conversation ran like this:

"You mean he's not *frum* (religious)?"

"Not *yet frum*."

"But I can barely speak a decent English."

"Speak from the heart."

"Yeah — but he is liable to ask me about God and that kind of stuff."

"Well, you do *daven* to Him three times a day, let alone learn His Torah."

"And what if he asks me about *emunah* (faith)?"

"Chances are you must have thought about that at least once in your life."

"All right, all right, but don't blame us if we make him '*frei*' (irreligious)."

"That's been taken care of already... He'll be over in half an hour; I hope you have an extra *kippa* in the house."

"Gulp..."

AND SO Shloime and Faigee received their first "guest from the Wall." They braced themselves for the worst but were still caught off guard when he shook Faigee's hand. Nervously they tried to make their guest (and themselves) feel at home. "Where are you from?" "Do you have any brothers and sisters?" "What brings you to Israel?" And with this last question they had basically exhausted all their prepared topics of conversation.

Yet it was only ten after seven and the meal had just begun. "By the way," Shloime remembered in a last desperate attempt, "what's your name?"

"Jerry."

"Do you know your Hebrew name?"

"Ahhh, Joshua."

"You mean *Yehoshua*. Joshua in Hebrew is Yehoshua. Do you know your father's Hebrew name?"

"If I remember correctly from my bar mitzva, his name is Levi."

"You're kidding. That means your name in Hebrew is *Yehoshua ben Levi*. Did you know that *Yehoshua ben Levi* is a very famous name?"

"Never heard it before."

"Why, I read about *Yehoshua ben Levi* every day of the week; he was a famous *ammorah* in the *gemorah*."

"What does that mean?"

"That means that you have the same name as one of the most famous rabbis who ever lived."

"C'mon."

"Really!"

"What's so famous about him?"

"What's so famous about him?! He was one of the smartest men who ever lived; he knew everything from the star constellations to all the laws of damages... Can you read Hebrew letters?"

"A little bit."

"Good, see for yourself."

Shloime removed a *gemorah Brachos* from the bookcase and showed Jerry a statement made by Reb *Yehoshua ben Levi*. He then opened a *gemorah Babba Kamma*, then a *Makkos; gemorah* after *gemorah*, finding the name *Yehoshua ben Levi*.

Jerry was so excited he couldn't contain himself. At first he started memorizing every one of the statements and then wanted to know all of the details pertinent to *Yehoshua ben Levi*'s comments.

Shloime was also excited, he had one of his first, and certainly most attentive student, lapping up his every word. Faigee was beaming with pride over her husband's pedagogic abilities. She kept winking at him as if to say, "You're such a pro!" Shloime tried to refrain from grinning so as to retain his scholarly and academic demeanor.

At 11:15 the two were still poring over the *gemorah*s when Shloime finally mustered enough resolve to deliver a proposal he never thought he would make. Looking as calm and objective as he could, he nonchalantly slung his arm over Jerry's shoulder and said, "You know, it is clear to me that you have unusual talmudic ability — just like your namesake. Who knows... maybe you are actually a descendant of Reb *Yehoshua ben Levi*? Don't you think you should give yeshiva a chance?"

Jerry smiled. "You mean if I go to yeshiva I'll know as much as you?" "There's no doubt about it," Shloime responded a bit abashed. "All you have to do is wish it — and we'll stand by your side, right Faigee?" "Our house is always open to you," she added.

And so, Jerry — *Yehoshua* — entered one of Jerusalem's *baal teshuva* yeshivas. Shloime and Faigee, now regular Shabbos hosts for beginners, realized that the pleasure and the *zechus* was all theirs.

WHEN THERE'S HOPE THERE'S LIFE

No one knows how many elderly Jews are abandoned by their families in slum neighborhoods. Lonely and miserable, they are a silent badge of shame on the Jewish community. The following is the story of one such Jew.

REB YANKEL Perchofvsky told me that if you could pull a plug from the bottom of Hudson Harbor, you would find it strewn with *tallesim* and *tefillin*. "Even on my boat, de Peta Stoivesant, dey thrown em ovabawd when dey seen de Statue of Liboity," he used to say. That's the way he talks, unless he reverts to his fluent Yiddish.

Reb Yankel often repeated the details of his trip to America for it was a bitter memory that he refused to forget. "Evebody said dat America iz anderish, diff'ent. Dey figged dey don't havva keep no mitzvas hea."

Our conversations rarely varied. He always started with the boat trip, the docking at Ellis Island and his employment on the Lower East Side of Manhattan. Maybe that's the way lonely old people are, they tell you the same story every time you visit.

REB YANKEL SET out for America to give his son a better life than that which could be expected in Russia. The

Perchofvskys waited seven years until David, their only child, was born. Their every hope had been invested in that little boy in the fervent wish that one day he might develop into a distinguished *talmid chacham*.

The local rabbis, however, viewed their plans differently: *"If you want to help Dovide'll, – if you really want him to become a talmid chacham, don't take him to that treifa medina,"* they used to say.

"But what future does he have in Russia?" Reb Yankel would reason. *"Even if I have to work 18 hours a day in America, Raizel, she should only be well, will be able to look after him every day when he returns from yeshiva."*

IN THE winter of 1912, Reb Yankel arrived in New York. A stranger in a frightening land, he was greeted by a second cousin who informed him at the outset that he could not expect family assistance or boarding.

It took two years of work to earn enough money to purchase a ticket for the wife and son that he had left in Russia. The outbreak of World War I in the fall of 1914 resulted in waiting another four years until he was finally reunited with Raizel and eight-year-old David.

Until their arrival Reb Yankel boarded with a Jewish family and worked on the docks. There wasn't a pier on New York's Lower East Side that Yankel didn't know. Every Friday he was fired from his job because he refused to work on Shabbos. He once managed to hold on to a job for almost four months because of his honesty, but when Polish immigrants showed that they were just as honest and never missed a day, this job also became another nick in his belt.

Few Jews had Yankel's perseverance. Even when his family arrived and expenses increased, Shabbos was Shabbos. He refused to accept the rationalization that *"America iz anderish"* as a way of life.

Reb Yankel's dream that Raizel would be free to take care of David turned out to be the kind of wishful thinking that could only have originated in Europe. The Perchofvskys were barely able to rent a one-room apartment on the fourth floor of an old building on Delancey Street, where Raizel started working. Tediously, she sewed countless pockets with a rented sewing machine that brought their weekly income to a total of nine dollars.

Raizel was a good wife. Though she had opposed the trip to America from the outset she remorsefully went along with Yankel's desire. It didn't take Raizel long to realize that America was anything but a *goldenna medina*. She never had time to look after David, let alone care for herself.

SIX YEARS after coming to America, Raizel died of pneumonia. She had complained about a shaking chill and fever and often veered off into delirium. The Perchofvskys couldn't afford coal nor could they afford the loss of income which would result from her being bedridden.

After Raizel's passing, Reb Yankel was adamant that David finally attend yeshiva. If David was not enrolled, how could he face the Almighty? How could he explain that he had abandoned the *shtetel* which cost his wife's life only to have David go to public school with *goyim*? David would never develop into a *talmid chacham* playing in the streets.

David, however, had other ideas. It is difficult to influence a child when you see him only once a week — aside from Shabbos, they never saw each other. David had already formed his group of friends, who were anything but yeshiva candidates. He didn't envisage himself remaining in school more than another year or two, anyway, before he would seek employment.

His father turned a deaf ear to all of David's objections to a yeshiva education. Protesting all the way, David was dragged over the bridge to Williamsburgh in search of a yeshiva. Reb Yankel and David had to wait a long time to meet with the principal of *Torah Vodaath,* who indicated at the outset that acceptance was out of the question. Yankel pleaded with the man. *"But he's a yasome and... and a shomer Shabbos...!... One day I hope I'll be able to pay tuition. I don't have the time to look after him, but here at yeshiva, at least the rebbeim will be able to care for him."*

The principal at *Torah Vodaath* was a kind and compassionate man. David was accepted, but as predicted, never proved to be an asset to the school. His mind was always on other things and he never appreciated the sacrifices that his father or the yeshiva made on his behalf.

After finishing tenth grade, David tried his hands at a number of trades until he met a second generation American girl who he married in 1935. Prior to World War II, they moved to Montreal and since then, David has all but forgotten about his father. He once offered to try and find him a nursing home, but he never did more than that.

EVER SINCE, lonely and deserted, Reb Yankel remains on New York's Lower East Side. He lives in a tenement on Madison Street that was probably never considered a decent building. The halls wreak of urine and are littered with discarded flyers, apple cores and marijuana stubs. The steps are beveled to an edge by the tread of countless feet, blackened beyond washing by the ground-in dirt of the area. Palms of sliding hands have buffed the cracked paint of the banister.

Like many other buildings in the East Side, this apartment house is a haven for junkies. The elderly who live there, most of them Jewish, live in constant fear within the very walls of their own homes. Reb Yankel must have put half a dozen new *mezuzos* on his front door before realizing that he could no longer afford the cost or the anguish of having them ripped off just hours after they were affixed.

Over the years Reb Yankel Perchofvsky's rheumatism has turned him into a cripple. In 1971, the City of New York assigned a welfare worker to his case. The first one stole a great deal of the little he owned and never locked the door when she left allowing the junkies who prowled the halls to steal most of what remained. When the City finally caught on to the delinquency of this worker, she was replaced with another who wasn't much better. At least the second one helped him out of bed and to the bathroom whenever he begged enough.

REB YANKEL is truly a Jewish hero. Today, there are few jobs that demand *chillul Shabbos* (desecration of the Sabbath); but when Reb Yankel Perchofvsky came to America, the idea of not working on Shabbos practically did not exist. Undoubtedly, he'll receive his reward for his fortitude — but not in this world.

When we visited him, we found a broken man: disabled, uncared for, waiting for the day that he would suffer no more.

Reb Yankel never really had a chance to learn. The little that he had studied in *cheder* was long forgotten. When he had the peace of mind and was able to balance a book on his knees, he would read his wife's *Tz'enah Ur'enah*. The stories in that book were so absorbing! But even so, his peace of mind was forever shattered by a vigilant conscience which always nagged —

> *"Why did he ever come to America? Was a pogrom ever as bad as what he was now suffering? His wife was content to stay in Russia, how he missed her now! Maybe David would have turned out differently over there..."*

Everyday he asked himself the same questions. Had he come to America to be at the mercy of a callous welfare worker? *"Someday,"* he told us, *"this loneliness will end."* What could we say? What solace could we offer him?

What could we offer him?! Far more than his son ever gave. Yankel Perchofvsky, and thousands of elderly Jews abandoned on New York's Lower East Side and dozens of other neighborhoods throughout the globe are decaying from isolation. Forsaken with nothing more than bitter memories, their loneliness eats into the soul.

Forgotten by their children, they wait only for the angel of death to relieve their suffering. A periodic visit to such a deserted Jew shows that someone cares, that life is worth living. And while there is life there is hope — and while there is hope there is life.

A Time to Rend

WHERE ARE THE SCARS

> *The Torah views history as the unfolding of the Divine plan and its study a holy imperative. The blasphemy of obfuscating and deliberately obliterating what happened in the past can, nonetheless, teach a sacred lesson.*

IN SOME WAYS, I still cherish memories of my boyhood visits to Vienna; how I walked the streets, rode the trolleys, and observed my fellow Austrians. One winter morning as I walked the cobbled streets, I slipped on the ice and knocked over an old man as I fell. Within a few seconds, this old gent had lifted me up, handed me my hat, and brushed off my snow covered shoulders. "*Gruss Gott,*" he said, and was on his way. I was impressed — a bonafide *mentsch.*

The next summer I visited Vienna again, and once more was exposed to Viennese *Mentschlichkeit:* I had descended from a trolley at Stepfansplatz, Vienna's main shopping hub, and was followed by a woman waving her arms. She presented me with a 100 shilling note which had fallen out of my pocket. Aside from the inherent kindness of her act, she now had to wait for another streetcar and pay the fare once more. I had never witnessed this on the I.R.T. Who doesn't like a *mentsch*?

Several years have elapsed between that summer and a recent winter visit. Since then, my affection towards Austrians has dwindled and my Jewish memory has expanded. I beheld more this time than I had formerly. Previously, every Austrian was my respected friend; now I kept asking myself that haunting question: *What was he doing during the war?* It occurred to me that the elderly man who had picked me up could be the very one who murdered my grandparents; and that the considerate lady may not have been kind at all during the war years — were the Austrians any better than the Germans? Both were united in their barbarism. Together they had succeeded in perverting any potential benefit to man: Their universities taught racial "science," their medicine employed virulent doctors, their chemistry invented Zyklon B gas. They assembled orchestras to drown out Jewish screaming.

I was living a paradox: I had witnessed their benevolence; I had studied their malevolence. My only comfort was in another contradiction. The characters are different but the dilemma is similar.

THE DIALOGUE between *Avraham Avinu* and Avimelech, King of Gerar, is rather perplexing: Avimelech took Sarah, Avraham's wife, assuming that she was his sister as Avraham had said. Avimelech's behavior was just as he put it: "In the innocence of my heart and the integrity of my hands I have done this" — scrupulous. When notified of his error, he speedily rectified the situation: "Avimelech took sheep and cattle and men servants and maid servants and gave them to Avraham, and restored Sarah his wife to him..." He asked in return merely the answer to a justifiable question: "In what way did I sin against you that you have brought upon me and my kingdom such a great sin? Deeds that ought not be done you have committed against me. What then did you see that you did this thing?"

Avraham Avinu's reply is, *prima facie*, puzzling. *"Because I said there is no fear of God in this place, and they will kill me on account of my wife."* Avraham had not responded to the question posed nor did he acknowledge

Avimelech's probity.

It was not until another visit to Austria that I could understand *Avraham Avinu*'s response and meanwhile reconcile my personal paradox. Of course Avimelech was kind, generous, probably well educated and highly cultured. One can talk like a *mentsch* and act like a *mentsch*; however, it can still be a deception. *Avraham Avinu* was not deluded. Pick me up when I fall down, return my money, present me with sheep and cattle. But as long as "There is no fear of God in this place," I am afraid for my life.

F ROM VIENNA, my wife and I drove 120 kilometers to Mauthausen, location of one of the most demonic death camps. No Jew survived there for more than three days. After their arrival the Jews were shunted into the adjacent quarry. They were not allowed to use the steps to the bottom of the pit, but had to slide down the loose stones on the side which killed and injured many before they even reached the bottom. The survivors then had to load each Jew with an excessively heavy rock which he was forced to run up the steps. In many cases the rocks immediately rolled downhill, crushing the feet of those behind. This slave labor insured quick liquidation as a result of overwork and starvation.

On their third day in the camp the S.S. opened the so-called "Death Gate" and with a fearful barrage of blows drove the Jews across the guard line where sentries in their watchtowers armed with machine guns shot them down in heaps. Camp prisoners were also murdered with phenol injections, bullets shot precisely into the nape of the neck — rendered feasible by means of a special measuring installation, and gas chambers.

T HE VILLAGE of Mauthausen looks like a picture postcard: white Alps form the backdrop of this quaint serene town. A steeple church stands at its center. As we approached the camp, we wondered how they would memorialize the destruction of hundreds of thousands of Jews? A question which has bothered me for years and catalyzed this trip.

Certainly no place was more appropriate to bemoan the loss of European Jewry than a concentration camp site. Here, for sure, the scars of guilt and feelings of contrition of the Germans and their Austrian allies would be apparent... Even those not directly involved in the mass murders were silent witnesses. This, too, demands some expression of mourning or remorse. At the entrance to the camp we stopped to read a sign indicating the death toll: there was a list of countries and a corresponding list of mostly five-digit numbers. We were surprised that the sign did not indicate that most of the people killed in Mauthausen were Jews.

I tried to open the gate but it was locked. "*Jahwohl, es ist zugespert,*" said the attendant from a window inside, — "*Winterurlaub.*" Winter vacation?! At a concentration camp? The Viennese Kunthistoriches Museums didn't have winter vacations...

SINCE THE camp was locked we went to the nearby memorial plaza. Every country whose Jews perished in Mauthausen was entitled to erect a memorial in their memory. The first monument we came upon depicted a man with his hands in the air, and bore an epitaph reading: "People be alert."...France had erected a memorial "*Aux Liberales,*"... Poland's monument paid tribute to the victory over Fascism... A Russian memorial consisted of a bare-chested muscle-bound warrior, with one arm huddling a girl and the other arm chained to the wall. It bore the inscription: "The victims of Fascism."...

Luxembourg had put up a small stone slab with only the word "Luxembourg" engraved on it... Albania erected a statue of an Albanian soldier overpowering a helmeted

S.S. soldier with the butt of his rifle. Germany, bizarrely enough, had the most ostentatious memorial. There was a stone relief of a heavy woman, surrounded by a brick wall. Hewn into the wall was a poem by Bertold Brecht:

> "O Deutschland bleiche mutter!
> Wie haben deine sohne dich zugerichtet..."
> O Germany pale mother,
> In what condition have your sons left you,
> That you sit amongst the peoples,
> A mockery or a fear.

WASN'T THERE a reminder of the thousands of Jews who had been annihilated? A hint, a trace, a suggestion? I then understood why the sign at the gate listed the losses of *Poles, Czechs, Finns,* as opposed to: *Polish Jews, Czechoslovakian Jews; Finnish Jews.* Austria, as well as her neighbors, refuses to recognize the Jews as a people and a nation. Therefore, it was Polish citizens who perished, not Jews. Is it not ironic that Jews earn citizenship posthumously? While Jews are denied equal rights during their lifetime and are the victims of venomous decrees, after their death they are dubbed citizens, and their particular Jewishness is totally obliterated.

We desperately searched for some acknowledgment. At the edge of the forest, beyond the memorial plaza something caught my eye: From the distance it looked like an ordinary tombstone a meter high. As we approached we discerned Hebrew letters. How apt — but why out here? Hewn into the marble were God's words to Cain who had just murdered his brother Abel: "The voice of your brother's blood cries out..." Several countries had elected to dedicate monuments to the victory over fascism. This memorial had been dedicated by *die Judische Jugend* in *Ostereich* (the Jewish Youth in Austria).

FOUR DAYS after our experience in Mauthausen, we took a bus from Prague to Theresienstadt (Czech: Terezin) to visit the remains of a ghetto which in the years 1941-45 held over 150,000 Jews. The Nazis deported Jews primarily from Western and Central Europe to Theresienstadt, in order to gradually transfer them to death camps, particularly Auschwitz. We got off the bus in Terezin next to an army camp and asked one of the sentries where the concentration camp was. He pointed nearby to an area which was filled with memorials and monuments. It appeared as if they did not forget to commemorate a single victim, a welcome change after Mauthausen.

We passed this vast area and headed towards the camp gate where Czech tourists were milling about. Inside the gate were maps and explanations in various languages describing what had transpired there. An attendant, noticing my skullcap and beard, pointed out in German that we were in the wrong place. This camp was used exclusively for political prisoners, we were probably interested in the "crematorium" which dealt with the Jews.

Asked whether there wasn't a crematorium in this camp, she replied, *"Nein."* This camp was for political prisoners; the only crematorium in Terezin is in the *Judische Konzentrationslager.* She gave us approximate directions how to reach the Jewish concentration camp (crematorium). As we walked through Terezin we pondered the painful realization that this village of 3,000 was inhabited years ago by 53,000 back-to-back Jewish inmates. We expected Theresienstadt to be restored like its hapless political counterpart.

WE WOULD NOT have found the crematorium had I not tripped over a railroad track almost buried by forty years of plant growth. We followed the track until it terminated, coinciding with our destination. No doubt this was the means of the heinous transports. The Jewish concentration camp was also crowded, but with a different assemblage: boys were racing, girls were giggling and women were strolling with their baby carriages. This wasn't a concentration camp — rather, a park, endless acres of green grass with plenty of shade. We beheld only four non-natural obstructions: A tiny white house with a chimney, an ornamented hammer and sickle, a concrete menora, and a large cross erected in someone's honor. But where was the camp? The gate? The crematorium, the barbed wire? Up on the embankment were some buildings encompassed by stone walls, we speculated that this must be the camp. We trudged through a manure covered field to discover that this was only a farm.

Theresienstadt sat below. My great-grandmother perished there, but one would never know. It was too pastoral and serene. A white house, hammer and sickle, a menora and a cross — that's all there is. The smoke stack of the white house should have given it away. Why would they paint such a nefarious building white? The front and back doors were locked. I was inflamed, my wife was speechless. Scribbled in the corner of a window was a note which read, "Closed since October '77."

Behind the crematorium was an interminable row of identical plain memorials erected by countries whose Jews were extinguished in Theresienstadt. There weren't any monuments or epitaphs, just monotonous grey slabs of concrete which bore the names of the countries. At the end of this row, in the furthest part of the park, we found a black and gold monument: — *"Lechavod Zichram* — in honor of the memory," read the memorial, "of the thousands of saints who perished here by the iniquitous Nazi regime... *Hashem yechonein efram.* — May the Almighty have mercy upon their ashes. — Erected by the Jews of Czechoslovakia." There weren't any attendants, any maps, any explanations... but we didn't need any — *Avraham Avinu* had already explained it.

ROSITA'S LEGACY

The tear-soaked pages of Jewish history are replete with little-known heroes and heroines. The stories of the vast number of saints and martyrs who perished in the sanctification of God's name, will never be told. Retelling the story of one such martyr provides an insight into the hundreds of thousands who had the fortitude to lead a similar life.

ROSITA ESCAPED the Spanish riots of 1391, but her parents were not as lucky. Elsa and Menachem de Silva perished that year along with tens of thousands of other Jews in the pogroms which decimated seventy holy communities in Castile and thirty-six communities in Aragon.

Already old at the age of eight, Rosita witnessed her neighbors attack her parents, while the priests and nobles ravaged her family's property. Jews who fought back were mercilessly slaughtered, her brothers among them.

Converts to Judaism were burned alive. Rosita's cousin, Francesca Homena and her four children served as a giant torch to the martyrdom of Israel. The same mob which ransacked the synagogue pillaged one Jewish home after another. At the same time, foreign sailors joined in the plunder, attaching themselves to the mob in order to rape the women and take part in the looting.

In just one afternoon, the thriving community of

Majorca vanished. Nary a sign of the years of Jewish residence remained: the Jewish school, like Rosita's home, was given to the monastery, and the Jewish cemetery was turned into a pasture for cattle.

WHEN THE TERRIBLE storm finally ended, Rosita was all alone. With her family and friends dead, she fled to Barcelona with some other wretched refugees. They travelled at night and hid during the day. And all they could find to eat was grass which failed to satiate their ravenous hunger. The cold gnawed at their bones, and they did not even have the consolation of knowing that they would eventually find a warm house or any other form of shelter. Without adequate clothing to protect themselves from the freezing weather, they were forced to lower themselves into holes they dug in the garbage that lined the roadside.

When Rosita finally reached Barcelona it was just a few decades before a larger horror which would ultimately engulf all of Spanish Jewry. Even at her tender age, Rosita understood that her sole obligation was to survive — to survive as a Jew. She knew instinctively that by surviving as a "Daughter of Israel" she would avenge her family's murder and perpetuate their memory. The task she set herself — surviving — was not a simple one.

NEVER UNDERESTIMATE the conviction and determination of a Jewish woman; not for nothing are they described as women of valor. Rosita was ready to take on the mighty Spanish empire if necessary. For one moment she didn't lose her faith. In the meantime, however, she attended a school that had been set up for refugees and dreamt about her future.

A month after her twenty-fourth birthday, Rosita married a man who had also been orphaned during the riots that destroyed her family and community. Two years later she gave birth to a son, Menachem, named after her father — and after the times. "May he only live up to his namesake," Rosita prayed. "Menachem — the comforter: may the Jewish people know no more suffering!"

It WAS a vain hope. Tranquility returned to the Jews of Spain for but a short while, and by the time Menachem celebrated the bar mitzva of his fourth son there was already talk of "heretics."

There were rumors that heretics would be punished — severely punished. But this did not daunt Rosita; she was too busy raising her grandchildren.

"We have no reason to be scared or ashamed," she comforted them. "We are the truly proud ones! God ordained that a Jew follow the Torah and trust in Him. If that means being called a heretic, so be it."

Rosita WAS spared the torment of living to see a repetition of her childhood. For, in a matter of months, the Inquisition swept the country. Torquemada and his henchman conquered the hearts of the King and Queen but failed to capture the Jewish soul. Menachem's sons and grandsons, like so many other Jewish boys, continued studying Torah, hoping that the danger that was seething would soon pass. They married and had children not just to fulfill the biblical commandment, but also to defy their enemies. One day, they fervently believed, the inquisitors would share the ignominious fate of their predecessors who were bent on destroying the Jews. At the same time, they were sure, Judaism would flourish.

As preparations were being made to greet the month of Adar, 1492, with joy and gladness, the decree of expulsion was promulgated. All the Jews gathered at the gates of the palace to plead against this decree, but it was to no avail. Not even the great and powerful Jewish statesman Don Isaac Abarbanel and Don Abraham Señor could revoke the perfidy. The decree was truth and reason was a lie.

On TISHA B'AV, the last Jews left Spain. Of these, 150,000 found their way to Portugal from where they would be expelled once again four years later; others travelled to Italy and Avignon, while some wandered as far as the Ottoman Empire. According to tradition, untold thousands sailed to the four corners of the globe. And there is no way of knowing how many of them drowned in the depths of the sea or what happened to those who eventually reached land.

Menachem's oldest grandson and family were among a group of 50,000 which fled to North Africa. He had been reared in the rich tradition of his great-grandmother, Rosita. It proved to be a legacy that stood him in good stead during the dreadful days and nights he spent crowded in a boat that was too small for so many passengers and not seaworthy for such a long voyage.

When a plague broke out on the ship, the captain forced his passengers to disembark on an uninhabited, rocky island. At almost the moment Menachem's grandson set foot on the island, a storm erupted and lightning struck his wife dead. Too sad to linger at that spot, he lifted up his two sons and started to walk inland. Each step heightened the strain on his exhausted, famished body, and when he could no longer endure the pain, his knees gave way and he collapsed. When he woke several hours later he discovered that both his children had died of hunger. Barefoot and dishevelled, whipped by the tempest which swirled about him, with matted hair, a bloated stomach and a broken heart, he lifted his hands toward Heaven and exclaimed:

"Lord of the Universe, I have escaped to this god-forsaken place so that I may serve You, fulfill Your mitzvos and sanctify Your name; but You are trying to make me abandon my religion. My God and God of my fathers, if You think that You can shake my faith, You are mistaken. I was born a Jew and so shall I die. You may inflict pain on me, remove that which is dear to me, bring me to the brink of despair, but it will not help – I shall forever believe in You!"

He gathered some earth and grass, covered his sons' bodies and continued on his journey.*

This immortal testimonial he inherited from Rosita and bequeathed to us.

---

* The story on the island was told and retold after the expulsion and is recorded in *Shevet Yehuda*.

MY JERUSALEM

> On the 28th of Iyar, 5742, Jerusalem celebrated the fifteenth anniversary of its reunification. Part of the festivities included an essay contest marking the end of Jerusalem as a divided capital. The following was the winning essay.

I HAVE been blessed with the curse of the Wandering Jew. Blessed — because wandering for me has meant walking the streets of my land and of my city. Wandering isn't an avocation without drawbacks. The loneliness of the veteran walker is inevitable. Imagination becomes one's only companion. For some this means Mitty-esque fantasies of political power, great wealth, daring... just minutes outside the door.

Such mental peregrinations have never suited me. The wanderings of my mind often interfere with the wanderings of my feet resulting in jaywalking, missed destinations, and collisions with lamp posts. Yet, walking in Jerusalem is an experience apart. I'm not referring to the ubiquitous hills, or the realization that walking will get you there quicker than waiting for a bus. Walking in Jerusalem, "my Jerusalem," is a spiritual rendezvous with the vintage Jewish experience.

JUST WALK the streets and read their names! Walking three blocks is not merely crossing Madison, Park, and

Lexington. It means going from *Hanevi'im*/Prophets Street to *Shivtei Yisrael*/Tribes of Israel Street to *Shmuel Hanavi*/Samuel the Prophet Street. How can one but feel history rush by! Each step is a leap into the past. *Rechov Hanevi'im*: Isaiah, Ezekiel, Jeremiah, this street is named after you! Who can think about traffic lights while engrossed in the message of days of yore? Isaiah's call to act righteously, seek justice, relieve the oppressed, judge the fatherless, and plead for the widow echoes through the street. Jeremiah's laments and Ezekiel's visions permeate the asphalt.

Walk up *Rochel Imainu* Street and try to feel lonely. It simply isn't possible. For thousands of years Rachel has been masterfully offering solace to lonely, wandering Jews.

Each street is nothing but a hint, a suggestion of a whole cast of spiritual heroes who share the road with me. Uninvited, they join me just the same, for my Jerusalem is theirs. I am a mere newcomer embarked on paths less spiritual and monumental.

GEOGRAPHICALLY, Abraham's trip here was shorter than mine, his baggage lighter. I brought a lift; he brought his one and only son as a sacrifice. Father Abraham's memory nags at me as I walk Jerusalem's streets looking for specials, and glancing at posters. His thoughts as he walked the same streets were what would happen to the future of the Jewish nation which he was about to sacrifice on the Temple Mount.

> An English tourist once stopped me on Mount Zion and asked if it was true that only a crusader was buried in "King David's Tomb?" I told her that I didn't know, but I was sure that where we were standing, **David had conversed with Jonathan** and not much further down the hill Solomon had written Proverbs. "In my opinion," I told her, "there's

sanctification enough in that!" (Perhaps she thought I was overzealous — but, after all, one tends to excess in guarding that which is precious).

WALKING on Mount Scopus I cannot help but recall Rabban Gamliel, Rav Elazar ben Azariah, Rabbi Joshua, and Rabbi Akiva. From this very lookout they beheld in the distance a fox emerging from the location of the "Holy of holies" in the freshly destroyed Temple. They could not bear the thought that a site so holy should be thus profaned. Am I not heir to their sensitivities?

Im eshkachaich Yerushalayim — If I forget thee O Jerusalem... It is so easy to live in this holy city and forget what a privilege it is to be here. The ease... how new it is! I try to maintain the vision of the elevated mien of the *Shtetel Yid* who saved up his rubles for twenty years solely to make the long, taxing journey to Jerusalem.

Imagine taking a walk with Yehudah Halevy. The experience could be either inspiring or depressing. His travails diminish the effect of the many *aliyah* stories which we love to tell. After all, we didn't really sacrifice that much to get here — giving up some luxuries, conveniences, a few thousand dollars, and boarding and deplaning. Contrast this with the story of Yehudah Halevy — what dedication, what sacrifice, what martyrdom! We are able to come, tour, enjoy, while he, at his very entry to this holy city, was cut down by that iniquitous rider.

And how about Moses Montefiore? How he loves to show me around the city! He has so much *nachas* from the way that it is built up. Sir Moses wants me to build too. Physically, spiritually, or emotionally, one must build in Jerusalem. London or New York may be suitable background for stagnation, but not Jerusalem! The students of the Vilna Ga'on, the Baal Shem Tov, and so many others throughout the centuries, came here to teach that same message.

Our brave soldiers complete my Jerusalem collage, joining ranks with my distinguished cortege. I don't need the unfortunately too-frequent memorials to lodge a lump in my throat. Dozens of pockmarked buildings are eternal testimony to the battles waged and the lives sacrificed in the struggle to liberate our city.

"SEEK the peace of Jerusalem," sang the Psalmist, a fervent prayer that no more blood be spilt to safeguard and preserve the "inner essence" of our nation. I fervently pray that "my Jerusalem" will be my children's Jerusalem, and the Jerusalem of all men able to dream and live in the tradition of this great city.

BIBLE ANYONE ?

Dozens of programs and hundreds of thousands of dollars are spent every year on attracting young men and women to come to Israel. Few are the programs that recognize or even attempt to acknowledge that Torah and Judaism are an integral part of the Israeli experience.

THE NUMBER eight (*shemona* in Hebrew), wrote the Maharal of Prague, is suprarational. Seven corresponds the number of days in a week; *shemona* lacks such conformance. Seven is indicative of rationality, eight of irrationality.

I lack a rational explanation for how I arrived at and what transpired in Kiryat Shemona (City of Eight). My reason for going, however, would score an even seven for its rationality: American Jewry is halving itself. Assimilation and intermarriage are raging epidemics. Yet the Jews of America do not even deign to offer their children the barest outlines of a Jewish education, to provide them with the least substantial reason for wanting to remain a Jew. And in Israel, those who have the power to make such an effort, to begin the task, do not even care.

Young Americans, most of whom think they came to Israel because they had no job, no marriage prospects, in short no reason for staying at home, in actuality came to find that reason for being a Jew. Of course, if you said that to most of them, they would laugh at you. "Jewish" to them means gaudy bar mitzvas, hot pastrami sandwiches and intrusive mothers whom they loathe. But show them the essence, not the accretions of an immigrant culture gone riot, and they will grasp it willingly.

The program for Americans at Kiryat Shemona, it seemed, was an opportunity to do a small bit to stem the tide. And under the circumstances, every opportunity is in truth an obligation.

While there is a general stereotype of the "typical *yeshiva bochur*" and his conventional way of doing things, I chose to pursue a rather unique course. I left Jerusalem for Kiryat Shemona, a dusty development town tucked away, and usually forgotten, in Israel's northeast corner bordering Lebanon and Syria, to lecture on Judaism to a group of American college graduates who were in Israel for a year on a Jewish Agency sponsored *"Sheirut La'am"* (Service to the Nation) program. *Sheirut La'am* brings young college graduates for a year of work in one of Israel's impoverished development towns.

THE FIRST phase of this *Sheirut La'am* program consists of three months at an *ulpan* in Kiryat Shemona. Unbelievably, the *Sheirut La'am* volunteers had been bussed there almost directly from the airport at Lod. They incongruously skipped the Jerusalem stop-over that every tourist makes. After witnessing this program for over two weeks, I could not accuse the Jewish Agency of acting with intelligence in setting up this itinerary, but it certainly reflects a practical approach.

Kiryat Shemona is a Development Town founded in 1956. The word "development" is an ingenious example of Israeli optimism: "underdeveloped" would be more accurate and would dispense with the false connotations of progress the former carries. Generally they are situated on the border or otherwise removed from the urban centers and are usually peopled by once religious Sephardi immigrants. Unfortunately their religious feelings, more cultural than transcendental to begin with, in most cases have long since evaporated. The standard of living and level of education and culture is far below the Israeli average; the standard of crime and violence correspondingly exceeds the norm.

Despite the efforts of the local Rabbi, Zephaniah Drury, and the recent opening of a *hesder* (paramilitary) *yeshiva*, Kiryat Shemona is almost devoid of religion. And as far as Judaism to which an American college graduate can relate, Kiryat Shemona is a vacuum. Fifty American college graduates deposited in the midst of a town of illiterate Iraqis and Moroccans, four-and-a-half hours away from Jerusalem. What on earth can the Jewish Agency have been thinking of?

INFLUENCING SOMEONE towards Jewishness is a difficult task and doing it against his perceived will, utilizing only cold intellectual techniques, makes the job even more formidable. As I learned, however, the local reality and the *ulpan* schedule would work to my advantage.

By the time I arrived, the *ulpan* students had long since exhausted the amusement possibilities of the town's swimming pool and two movie theaters with their Turkish adventure epics. They had only three hours of classes in the morning. The afternoons and evenings were free, save for weekly Israeli dancing and sporadic lectures. The kids were so bored that a class on basket weaving would have been well-attended.

Accommodations at the *ulpan* had been kindly arranged for me by Rav Drury. Upon my arrival in Kiryat Shemona I went directly to the *ulpan* and made my presence known. The manager informed me that there were no accommodations prearranged. Rav Drury, he explained, did not and could not commit anything in the *Sheirut La'am* program. Furthermore, he said, a lecturer on Judaism was not needed (i.e. wanted) because there were hardly any Americans in the *ulpan*. The building, he assured me, was almost entirely inhabited by Argentineans and female soldiers.

I was shocked and hurt. I thanked him for his "hospitality," took my suitcase and walked to the Drury house. The Rabbi's wife verified that her husband had indeed spoken with the *ulpan* housemother concerning my housing.

THAT EVENING I returned to the *ulpan* to determine my status. This time I found the office attended by a boy — apparently local talent. I deduced that after office hours the Jewish Agency staff returned to their homes outside of Kiryat Shemona. I started "schmoozing" with this boy about the soccer standings and the like. Nonchalantly I inquired if the *ulpan* had any Americans. "*Betach* (of course)," he said, "Fifty-two Americans!" God of the Universe! I was stupefied. I questioned the feasibility of lecturing to them that very evening. He said that he was unacquainted with these matters and a *madrichah* (a female group leader) must be consulted. Since I was not allowed past the office, he offered to go up the stairs and inquire for me.

I was, I am ashamed to admit now, convinced that the *madrichah* would be delighted with the idea of having a volunteer lecturer on Judaism at the disposal of the students. They had already been in the *ulpan* for one month and so far had not heard or experienced anything about their religion. No attention was given to bolstering the weak Jewish backgrounds of the majority of the young Americans recruited. Every opportunity to infuse some spiritual values into the three-month intensive Hebrew course was passed by in favor of propagandistic attempts to lure the participants into permanent immigration.

I waited a long time for the *madrichah* to descend. Finally the boy came down alone. His disposition towards me was distinctly less affable. He relayed, in the name of the *madrichah*, the opinion that, *"None of the Americans are interested in Judaism."* The message and the manner she chose of delivering it spoke volumes.

THE ALMIGHTY has labeled us a stiff-necked people and who am I to diverge from our tradition? I asked the first three students I saw if they would be interested in a class on the basic elements of Judaism. The first student answered, "Sure," the second one affirmed more enthusiastically, and the third one even more so.

I was in business. That evening I taught the story of Rabbi Akiva: how a forty-year-old base shepherd molded himself into the greatest scholar of all time. I related the *Midrash* of how Moses, when given a glimpse into the future, marvelled at Rabbi Akiva's achievements, and how his students and generations of Jews have been inspired by his martyrdom. As I recounted the stories I witnessed the resurgence of a genuine feeling for Jewishness that I knew they must have had.

At first the students had been skeptical, assuming that the administration of the *ulpan* had coordinated the lecture. True, I had advertised Judaism, but they still expected to hear about Zionism, politics or development towns. When they realized that this was something entirely different, for them unique, their eyes lit up and they moved their chairs closer. The boy who had brought a newspaper into the class folded it under his chair; the girl who had brought her needlepoint stuffed it back into her bag. *"Rabbi who?" "Isn't Rabbi Akiva the name of a street?" "Moshe Rabbenu?!"* Even the cynics were friendly. *"I don't believe it, but it's a lovely story...*" And so Torah was introduced to the Kiryat Shemona *ulpan*.

THE NEXT MORNING, I spoke with the housemother about my accommodations. She denied speaking with Rabbi Drury; perhaps she had forgotten, perhaps she had been asked to forget, perhaps... In any event, accommodations were out.

I then inquired whether the *ulpan* was stocked with Bibles which could serve as my text. *There weren't any.* "Why?" *Because there isn't any interest in them, nor can the budget cover them.* But there were funds for an Israeli dancing teacher, daily delivery of the *Jerusalem Post*, and a television. *Lack of interest...*

Stiff-necked I was and stiff-necked I am and I insisted that the book-closet be unlocked and checked. When the closet was opened, we found twenty-five Bibles stacked inside. Blessed be His name, not just Bibles, but Bibles in English! My joy, however, was short-lived. I inspected them and I was stunned; twenty-five missionary Bibles, "Old" Testament and "New."

I imagine that a more conventional yeshiva student may have disposed of them on the spot. I had more faith than that. I wanted to explain to the *madrichot* the nature of the outrage, hoping that they would get rid of them on their own. I don't believe I ever had a less productive conversation in my life. *"Ma pittom, get rid of them? Maybe the Americans want to read them."* Said I: *"If the Americans want to read missionary literature, no one is stopping them, but why seduce them? The only literature in English save aliyah material is missionary Bibles. Our Bible you don't have, but theirs* (lehavdil) *you do have! Where is the sense?"*

One *madrichah* then said, *"We received these Bibles for free, and we never throw out anything we get for free."*

> "What kind of reasoning is this? If you were to receive an explosive for free would you keep it? Of course not! You'd throw it out before it explodes. What's the difference between physical harm and spiritual harm? Anyway," I added, "you threw out a lecturer on Judaism you got for free!"

I later smuggled twelve missionary Bibles out of the *ulpan* and took care of them myself. The housemother had collected the remaining Bibles in a box and assured me that she would take care of them. On the day I left Kiryat Shemona I pleaded with the head of the *ulpan* to make sure that such literature would never again gain entry. Out of curiosity I asked what was done with the Bibles. He told me that they were sent to a kibbutz in the area. If only we had such strong-willed people on our side...

THE MISSIONARY Bibles were out of the way, but the class did not have texts. I decided to take my appeal to the director of studies at the *ulpan*. I was informed that the only possible time to speak with him was during the coffee-break, when all the teachers and *madrichot* gathered in his office. As I waited to enter I overheard their opinions of me and of what I represented. If there had been a popularity poll I would have beaten Yasir Arafat — barely. I had thought, at first, that I was being hypersensitive and over-reacting to the situation, but now I knew for sure. It was clear that in their minds I was a spiritual malaise who had already succeeded in delivering one mildly poisoning lecture and must be curtailed.

I walked in, and politely inquired about the accessibility of Bibles. One teacher told me that he had Bibles, but he, to his regret, was unable to lend them to me, for he used them every morning in class. (I later found out from his students that he had never used them in class.) I pointed out that since he taught in the morning, an overlap was impossible, as I would never start teaching before mid-afternoon. While admitting the justice of my argument, he expressed the fear that his Bibles would get scattered and that some might disappear. I assured him that I was devoutly in favor of getting the maximum usage out of the Bibles and that he could be genuinely confident that they were in good hands. He finally acquiesced.

AT LAST we began. With the Almighty's help the classes progressed nicely and their effects soon became manifest. After the first week, two girls went to Jerusalem for Shabbos and returned enthused. I had the unparalleled joy of watching my students absorb Torah as a sponge might soak up water. But that's not to say that the harassment did not continue...

The lectures were held in a classroom adjacent to the maintenance room. On more than one occasion the noise emanating from there forced us to switch rooms. In one instance when the noise was particularly disturbing some investigation revealed a *madrich* pounding on a scrap of metal to be the responsible party. We asked him if what he was doing needed to be done right then? He replied that he was repairing something necessary for eating and it could not be delayed. *"Could you wait 15 minutes until we finish? – Anyway, the kitchen's empty and the next meal is in five hours... Furthermore, our tradition teaches that man does not live by bread alone but rather on what emanates from the mouth of the Lord."* Said he, *"I have no choice and you must understand."* We understood very well... We must have been more effective than we had imagined.

AFTER A WEEK of classes I asked when the most convenient time would be for delivering a lecture on the upcoming Rosh Hashanah holiday. The students were instructed to verify the suggested date with a *madrichah* and to publicize the event. The lecture was scheduled for eight o'clock Sunday evening and by Wednesday afternoon posters were already up. I spent Shabbos in Jerusalem and arrived early Sunday evening to make sure that everyone was aware of the talk. At supper one of my students announced the lecture, inviting everyone, including the *madrichot*. By seven forty-five the lounge was full; even some female soldiers posted nearby had come to listen. *Nachas mamash* — all these people so remote from Judaism gathered to find out about Rosh Hashanah.

Just as the talk was about to begin, a *madrichah* informed us that the lecture was cancelled due to the arrival of a guest lecturer from Beit Shean, a development town one-and-a-half hours south of Kiryat Shemona. The speaker had apparently been scheduled to speak well before the Rosh Hashanah lecture had been booked. I was told that I might speak after she had finished, two-and-a-half hours hence.

I believed that with some good will and reason we might have agreed on a compromise. Our talk was scheduled to last only forty-five minutes. *Perhaps, if I could speak with the lecturer from Beit Shean, we could work something out.*

I could see that my request touched a chord that brought the whole cauldron of simmering rage to the surface. *"You aren't wanted here,"* the *madrichah* retorted. *"Haven't you realized that yet? I know the students are more interested in Rosh Hashanah than Beit Shean. If you speak at the same time, no one will attend her talk. If you speak first, they will all be too tired to attend another lecture. What can I say to a woman who came all the way from Beit Shean? I told you in the beginning that you must confirm all your classes with me."*

I begged to correct her. She had never told me to confirm my classes, but rather had sent a message that, *"None of the Americans are interested in*

Judaism." I pointed out that I had come all the way from Jerusalem, three times further away than Beit Shean. *"Why,"* I asked, *"for the past four days had no one been notified of the conflict? – or at supper, for that matter? What is more important, Beit Shean or Rosh Hashanah?"*

> *You refuse to understand that you are not wanted. There is no room for Judaism in the* ulpan *– no room for God.*

The priorities were clear. Beit Shean had it over Rosh Hashanah. One *madrichah* insisted that despite it all, she respected God very much. *"Yofi,"* said I, though I rarely speak in His name.

Although it was difficult for them to sit for three consecutive hours, thank God their thirst for Torah won out. At 10:15 that night a sermon was delivered on Rosh Hashanah and the meaning of *teshuva.* For the duration of the sermon, the *madrichot* stood in the back — chatting, giggling, and disrupting. It was hard to be resentful, because they were obviously bemoaning their defeat.

T HERE IS a lot to write about concerning the *ulpan* in Kiryat Shemona. For the *Yomim Noraim* (Days of Awe) the students were farmed out to non-religious kibbutzim where the holidays were all but ignored. When they toured the Galilee, they stopped at every minor marker of a military victory, but for a brief stop at a site of religious significance there was "no time."

There is more than apathy at work, there is unnecessary hostility. Tisha B'Av, the fast day commemorating the destruction of our Temples, was selected as the time to teach the names of food — and each class was equipped with the appropriate edibles to aid in the instruction.

Here in the first truly Jewish environment many of

these sadly archetypal American Jews had experienced, they saw religion scorned at every turn. What do they think, those people from the Jewish Agency whose job it is to build a home for the Jewish people? Do they really believe that a state could be maintained by de-Judaized Jews? Can they not see beyond their ideological blinders that the way to attract disaffected American youth to Israel is not to offer them more of the sterile, atheistic universalism they have already rejected at home, but by giving them the spiritual ties they need and crave to the land and its people? Already more than ninety percent of American *olim* return to the States, beaten and frustrated after a few years in Israel. What will it take to make them see the light?

IT IS related in the name of the Chofetz Chaim that in the world to come the non-observant Jews will point their fingers at their religious brethren and justly accuse them of neglecting their brothers and sisters. How could we let Kiryat Shemona happen? What are we going to do to stop it? And if not now, when?

OHR SOMAYACH FURLOUGH

Since its inception, the Ohr Somayach Yeshiva in Jerusalem has attempted to reach out to every segment of Jewry. The desire to remind Jews of their heritage has taken Ohr Somayach representatives all the way from weekend retreats in New York to lectures in Australian outback towns. But what more natural place is there to reach Jewish hearts than at home in the Israeli army?

THE STRENGTH of the Israel Defence Forces lies in its soldiers; the strength of the soldiers lies in their motivation and morale. Accordingly, the Israeli army has the strongest Education Department of any army in the world.

It is in the halls of the Education Department and the lawns of its seminary retreats that the true battle is fought. And no one is spared from the front. At a day's notice, Israel's top professors and personalities can be drafted to deliver a lecture on any given topic.

OVER THE YEARS, the IDF Education Department has been re-assessing its strategy. The process began in 1974 when Paul Laster, an assimilated Virginian, took up a senior position in the Education Department. Laster was soon promoted to the rank of captain and a great deal of power was put at his command.

His job was to coordinate a one-week course offered to all army officers about the problems of Israeli society. The only difficulty was that the new captain could not see the sense in such a program: "What can be gained by learning about problems without offering solutions? How can such study bolster morale and strengthen the army?" he asked.

Laster took the dilemma to his superiors. The problems between Ashkenazim and Sephardim, the growing deficit in balance of payments and the strike-prone labor unions would do little to inspire a Jewish soldier to die for *Eretz Yisrael*, he reasoned. The way to reach a Jew, he ironically contemplated for the first time in his life, was through Judaism.

Laster's contemplation resulted in a new, seven-day course built around three ideas: Jewish identity, peoplehood and culture. Paul Laster realized that merely teaching or intellectualizing about Judaism would never have the same effect as an environment which would force his troops to confront their Judaism. But where could he take them? A yeshiva would be the ideal venue, but those he had heard about in Jerusalem and Bnei Brak would generate more ridicule than challenge.

THROUGH AN ARTICLE in *The Jerusalem Post*, he learnt about the Ohr Somayach Yeshiva in Jerusalem, where he quickly scheduled a meeting. It was a meeting that shattered every stereotype he ever had about rabbis and the yeshiva world. Intead of old European rabbis with heavy accents and narrow minds, he encountered quite the opposite. One dean he met had done his graduate thesis on a topic similar to his own; another was equally articulate and is a renowned author in the Anglo-Saxon religious world.

The deans had no qualms about allowing army officers visit the yeshiva, and, indeed, suggested various lectures, topics and programs they could offer to the soldiers.

The idea of bringing high-ranking army officers (the lowest rank of those attending the one-week course is lieutenant) to a yeshiva raised some eyebrows in the military establishment, but Laster's superiors let him have his way.

THE FIRST GROUP of army officers to visit Ohr Somayach participated in an intensive day of study and observation. Their program included a movie, special lectures, workshops, a brief *chavrusa* set-up and a tour of Ohr Somayach's Israeli division — the showpiece of the yeshiva. All of the Israelis at Ohr Somayach served in the army and many still maintain important positions in the military. The students obviously preferred investing their spare time in the yeshiva's studyhall over a recreation hall or PX. At the end of the evening refreshments were served in the dining room. And there a surprise was in store for the officers...

When the officers walked in for coffee and cake, they encountered a familiar face smoking a cigarette in the back of the room.

"Who are you?"
"*Ma zeh mishaneh*" — what difference does it make?
"What's your name?"
"*Ma echpat licha*" — what do you care?

And then one of the officers identified the once famous face, now covered with a beard and topped with a *kipa*. "You're Ika Yisraeli!" (Israel's number one social butterfly and glamor boy).

Ika lit another cigarette. "What are you doing here?" he asked gruffly. And with that, an all-night discussion began, providing the army officers with just the kind of challenge which Captain Paul Laster was seeking for them.

THE SUCCESS and benefits of these initial programs began to spill over to non-commissioned officers and to the ordinary foot soldier. One *rav zvai* (army chaplain) after another started contacting Ohr Somayach to see if he could bring his troops for a visit.

Now, over 2,000 officers and soldiers — both men and women — pass through Ohr Somayach's doors each year. Female soldiers receive special attention from students at Neve Yerushalayim, the women's division of Ohr Somayach.

But all this does not mean that there haven't been any snags. Certain echelons in the army felt uneasy at the growing affinity displayed toward Ohr Somayach. Paul Laster, who had instigated the program — and had become religious in the process — anticipated his reassignment: he resigned.

The rumblings became so loud that the army's Chief of Manpower dropped by to see the yeshiva. He discovered that the rumors which had catalyzed his visit were clearly fabrications of a hateful mind, and he gave his wholehearted approval for the continued interaction between the army and Ohr Somayach.

COMMON IS THE story of a certain gutsy *rav zvai* who called Ohr Somayach with an unusual request. He is the *k'tzin da'at* (senior chaplain officer) at a paratroop base where commandos are trained. A new commando unit under his aegis was to be on "alert" that coming Shabbos. "Alert" is an army term which means that the unit must, at a moment's notice, be ready to enter combat, cope with a terrorist incursion or quash a disturbance in the territories. They sleep in their boots with their rifles at their side. As long as the unit is ready for action, it doesn't matter where it is located.

"Could Ohr Somayach," he asked, "absorb 85 commandos for Shabbos?"
"Ah... affirmative," was the reply.

On Friday afternoon, three buses laden with soldiers and their gear arrived at the yeshiva. It was a frightening sight to see them descend from the buses. The soldiers were armed to the teeth with hand grenades, missiles, rocket launchers, rocket-propelled grenades, rifles, walkie-talkies, helmets, tents, food, battle rations, personal gear... each backpack weighed more than 50 pounds. The troops were eighteen years old; the commanders were twenty and twenty-one and already veterans of Operation Peace for Galilee.

Their first instructions from the Ohr Somayach army liaison (none other than newly employed Paul Laster), was for them to select a basketball team — the Ohr Somayach varsity was already waiting for them on the courts adjacent to the yeshiva. Ohr Somayach wanted the first encounter to emphasize those elements which both groups shared in common, and provide the soldiers with a little recreation.

The captain of the yeshiva basketball team was a graduate in criminology from the University of Maryland, a dan-II black belt in karate and a volunteer in the IDF. He had spent the year before he entered the yeshiva as a soldier on the Beirut-Damascus highway, and the Israeli commanders were his "battle buddies" from Lebanon. The rapport between the men was thus warm from the outset.

IT DIDN'T take long for the Americans to blow the Israelis off the court. Among the doctors, lawyers and physicists which Ohr Somayach numbers in its ranks, it also has several all-state basketball players. But the Israelis had their sweet revenge a little later when they humiliated a group of green Americans on the soccer field. Before defeat seemed imminent, the Americans sent a delegation to the yeshiva dormitory to tap Ohr Somayach's international connection, and students from Uruguay, Britain, Holland, South Africa, Australia and New Zealand tried to save their languishing comrades.

At the Shabbos table a few hours later, Ohr Somayach changed the image of *kfiah datit* — religious coercion, which the soldiers had been reared upon. There was no pressure on the soldiers. The yeshiva students, their tables bedecked with especially delicious food and adorned with bottles of Coca-Cola, were warm and friendly. None of them were forced to attend yeshiva. They had all come from non-religious homes and had abandoned careers, girlfriends and beach-combing to devote their attention to Torah pursuits and study.

THE SOLDIERS and students exchanged jokes and thoughts. The language barrier was overcome with gestures, good cheer and occasional translators. And the spirit was electrifying. The *rabbeim* Ohr Somayach arranged to attend and conduct the meal and ensuing program were all lively, had good voices and wore *streimlach*.

Israelis love to sing. They don't have the hang-ups and inhibitions that Americans have about group expression. So the soldiers, students and *rabbeim* sang and sang. The dissonance of the various backgrounds harmonized into unison — melody which was translated into words in the talk which followed the meal.

On Shabbos morning, the soldiers divided into pairs to eat with families who live near the yeshiva. But the climax of Shabbos came at *seuda shlishis*, which was held in the yeshiva's main dining room. Singing turned to dancing as soldiers and students locked arms. And even when Shabbos was over, the fervor in the dining room was still at a high pitch. Guitars appeared and the dancing took on a new passion.

THE LOCKED arms between the soldiers and students

broke only once in order to exchange headgear — the students donning red berets, while the soldiers tried on black hats. The Ohr Somayach liaison was thrown on a chair and carried through the air by an ecstatic and grateful corps of troops.

Meanwhile, new Ohr Somayach recruits, who had been directed to the yeshiva the previous week by solicitors at the Western Wall, bus station and university campuses, were also benefiting from this emotional experience. The beauty and candor of it all highlighted the splendor of the yeshiva experience. It was also having an effect on the yeshiva veterans. Their novice feelings of incompleteness in Judaism evaporated as soon as they found themselves in the position of being religious role models for the soldiers.

That Shabbos also had an effect on the military establishment: "תודה רבה שהשרשתם יהדות בחיילנו" — "Thank you so much for instilling the values of Judaism in our soldiers," wrote one army colonel. "You have proved that yeshivas don't brainwash, but inspire," wrote another.

Yoav Tzur, a graduate of *tichon hachadash* (ultra-leftist high school in Tel Aviv), Peace Now activist and participant in the Shabbos, later confessed in a letter: "Ideologically, I am very far from you, but when I was with you I felt closer to you than I do to my own colleagues..."

Perhaps the greatest tribute of all came from the soldiers themselves. A few months later the groups deliberately detoured from the path of their march to stop at Ohr Somayach: "We just wanted to come by and say hello to our friends — and to say thanks again..."

MARKING THE CONCLUSION OF A BEGINNING

Neve Yerushalayim is a seminary for baalos teshuva – assimilated women exploring their Jewish roots. Neve Yerushalayim, and schools like it, try to instill their students with a dedication to the Jewish people and a commitment to Jewish law. Conventional teaching methods are not always able to achieve these goals.

NOT TOO LONG ago a celebration took place virtually unknown to the outside. The occasion was the completion of *Chumash Bereishis*. For most Jews, finishing *Bereishis* conjures up merely saying "*Chazak chazak...*" and continuing on to *Shmos* the following week.

For over 200 American *baalos teshuva* attending Neve Yerushalayim College for Women in Jerusalem, reviewing the Torah portion was the most intriguing, exhilirating and demanding exercise of their lives. To many of these girls "Judaism" itself was new, let alone the details of the Torah.

How do you teach *Chumash Bereishis* to a 25-year-old biochemist who never heard of Abraham and Sarah? This is a question Neve Yerushalayim has grappled with since its inception. The answer, more or less, is to start with the concepts and gradually lead the student into the text. Language skills are always a problem, but with the proper inspiration and instruction it's a temporary problem conquered in a matter of months, if not weeks.

Neve Yerushalayim decided to present the girls with a

new incentive to understand the weekly *parsha* (Torah portion) aside from the daily *parsha* class. The gimmick? *Parsha* assignment sheets, *parsha* tutors and a weekly *parsha* review — not unlike the study aids used in seminaries the world over, yet unusually ambitious for these girls. They took to the venture with a drive never envisioned by the school's administration. Rashi became the local hero. He was talked about before class, after class, during lunch and in the dorms. Woe to the teacher who was stumped on the location of a particular Rashi!

As THE end of *Bereishis* drew closer, a competition was planned between the school's various levels in conjunction with a *siyum* on the entire *Chumash Bereishis*. The week before the *siyum* the school was afire. Every teacher worked with his class with thorough exactness in preparation for the "Neve Bowl." Girls pulled "all nighters" recalling the weeks before "finals" in their college days. The finest yeshiva students would have profited by emulating the diligence that abounded during that grueling week.

> "When did Sarah give birth?"
> "Well, it's a maklokee, either Rosh Hashanah or Passover."
> "It can't be a maklokes, Rabbi Abramov said Sarah gave birth on Rosh Hashanah."
> " 'Zat so? Rashi says it was when the sun came a year later to the same spot, and Avraham had served the guests matzos!"

THURSDAY, the day of the competition, was a special day at Neve. The bulletin boards in every classroom, in the student lounge, and in the hall all had reminders about the *siyum*, but reminders were hardly necessary. At 10:15 in the morning the classes started filing into the specially decorated dining room. The tables were adorned with

Shabbos tablecloths, flowers and (a rare treat) bottles and bottles of Coca Cola.

The girls sat according to their levels *a la* "College Bowl."

"The first question is for level four: What blessing did Eisav receive?"

"He will dwell on the fat of the earth and have the dew from heaven, he will live by the sword and serve his brother!"

"One point for level four."

Yeah! Hooray! Thunderous applause. Posters and flags with no. 4 on them were waved back and forth.

"The next question is for level two. Level two are you ready?"

"Yeah! Hooray! Let's hear it for level two!!" Clap, clap, cheers!

"Where did Devorah die and why was it given that name?"

"Alon Bachus, oak of weeping, because Yaakov learned of Rivka's death there."

"One point for level two."

Yeah, yeah, clap, clap!

"Level one, what is the symbolism of the weight of Rivka's nose ring?"

"It represents the half shekel the Jews donated when they were counted."

Cheers upon cheers.

It was organized pandemonium.

And so it continued between the four levels, round after round. Applause and tense emotions and... and it was impossible to stump them. After 14 rounds not one level had made an error — it was a total deadlock.

THERE WAS just so long the contest could go on, and there were just so many questions that even the most knowledgeable teacher could ask. And so after a huddle of the referees (the four "level" heads), which took only two minutes but seemed like half an hour to the impatient audience, they decided that the winner was — everyone. It was an absolute tie. *Yeah, hooray,* applause. Awards were presented to all of the contestants: a painting of the Chazon Ish adorned by one of his quotations,

אין כל עצב בעולם למי שמכיר אור האורות של האמת

—"There is no depression for one who recognizes the light of the ultimate truth."

The presentation of awards was followed by a guest speaker who had come specially to participate in the *siyum*. He spoke about Torah and about life, or more specifically, "Torah is life."

> *"In the dark hours of World War II,"* he started, *"Winston Churchill told the citizens of Britain 'I have never promised anything but blood, tears, toil and sweat.' He didn't offer central heating in the trenches or conscription deferments to finish college – only blood, tears, toil and sweat. The English didn't look for a way out of the fight for they realized that Churchill was actually offering them life. That's right, life, for if the Nazi monster could not be contained, then life under it would not be worth living."*

The parable was clear — blood, tears, toil and sweat was life; such is the life of Torah, otherwise it isn't worth living.

> *"There are two ways to learn Torah,"* he continued. *"There's a story about a simple farmer who one day saw workers disturb the peace of his county by laying down long strips of metal. He had no idea what the strips were for until one day he was awakened from his nap by the reverberations in his house. In the distance a large steel object belching black smoke was inching out of the horizon. He stood between the rails to get a better view of the approaching strange hulk.*

As it drew nearer, he discerned a driver sitting up front who stuck his head out of the window and started waving at the farmer. The farmer returned the gesture by waving back at the engineer. In desperation the engineer leaned out the window waving frantically and yelling at the farmer to get off the tracks. Hearing nothing but the roar of that incredible locomotive, the farmer jumped for joy at all of this attention and waved back as hard as he could. The train chugged closer and closer and..."

"So it is," the Rabbi pointed out, *"you can be spoken to, waved at, yelled at, and hear nothing. There are,"* he repeated, *"two ways to learn Torah – you can walk out of a class and marvel at the stories and the teacher's delivery, or you can let the words penetrate your heart and realize that what is called for is blood, tears, toil and sweat!"*

The girls heard the message, and realized... *Chazak, chazak, venis'chazeik!*
"We accept, we shall be strengthened!"

It was a genuine *kabbalos haTorah*. For many, just weeks in the school, it was truly *naaseh venishma*.

The speaker sat down and the students were treated to a repast, a *seudas mitzva*, the likes of which Neve Yerushalayim or many other religious institutions have rarely seen. The tutors and *madrichot* (counselors) were the waitresses who graciously served their students who so deservedly earned this feast.

THE CEDARS OF LEBANON

Operation Peace for Galilee has been Israel's most agonizing and protracted war. Countless tragic reports of attacks and ambushes have only dulled our appreciation of the magnitude of each and every loss. Below is the story of just one of the fallen.

BY THE TIME the front line units had captured Damour, their strength was sapped and their nerves frazzled. In just four days they had covered over 80 kilometers through enemy fire, mines, and house-to-house combat. Beirut lay ahead.

Early Thursday morning, the fifth day of the war, they were given some time to rest.

"Noam, lie down already!" yelled his comrades and commander. But Noam Yehudah had other things on his mind.

The belt of a combat soldier, especially one from the Engineering Corps, is laden with all types of military paraphernalia. Noam's was equipped with a special pouch containing pocket-size *sefarim*. No matter how exhausted, Noam always consulted his pouch.

There wasn't all that much time to rest or learn. Soon the Air Force would finish its job and they would be ordered to roll ahead. Awaiting them was the last stretch of the coastal highway before the Beirut International Airport.

The crack Syrian infantry and the last strong contingent of the terrorists outside of Beirut were entrenched on both sides of the road. For some of the boys, this would be a one-way trip; topographically and strategically it was an uphill battle.

At 11:10 the command to move out was issued. Noam had put away his *sefarim* and was feeding a baby rabbit he had found in the field. Eighty kilometers north of the Israeli border, Noam gazed at the defenseless creature with a sense of *deja-vu*: as a child he had tended a white lamb abandoned by its mother in the Galilean hills near his home in Safed. Now he was worried about a rabbit deep into Lebanon — a shepherd would never allow his flock to wander into a battlefield. Moshe and Dovid were also shepherds when they were young; it's the vocation of the compassionate.

THERE IS NOTHING more awesome than riding off to battle, your heart commutes between your feet and your chest — your whole life flashes before your eyes. Forty-two tons of half-track and the cold steel of an automatic cannon between your palms offer no security or relief. Deep down you know that just one missile, one small RPG, or one hidden land mine and you're gone.

Soldiers flashed signals to each other. If you had a final message to tell a comrade, it was too late now. The noise of the tank column was like a jackhammer in stereo. The headphone intercom could only be used for orders. It was thumbs up all along the column, soldiers gritted their teeth and scanned the horizon. Noam was absorbed in thought.

Deeply religious, Noam thought he had a higher duty when he had joined the IDF. Noam was out to change the army. During basic training he served as the conscience of his military base. He objected to the assignment of stretcher-bearer as a "penalty;" tending the wounded is a privilege, he reasoned, and should never be associated with punishment. Private Yehudah's protest was brought to the attention of the base commander, who forwarded it to the upper command, who forwarded it to the Chief of Staff until... army policy was changed.

When conducting house searches in the territories, he ensured that belongings and furniture were never disturbed or damaged. He chastised soldiers overcome by temptation, and they honored his ethics.

He was one of the few non-commissioned officers who commanded respect, not just obedience. At his Engineer Corps base where few knew a soldier by name, everyone knew and loved Noam.

But his base and the army were just steppingstones in Noam's campaign to better the world. He rejected the notion of a "secular Jew." Noam saw each Jew as an individual who must be awarded the appropriate attention and respect. To find the means of narrowing the schism between all Israelis was a challenge that nagged him constantly.

THERE WAS little time to cogitate now. A *tefillah* crackled over the field radio:

> "*Shema Yisrael,* you draw near today to battle your enemies. Let not your hearts be faint, fear not, and do not tremble, nor be terrified because of them, for the Lord your God goes with you to fight with you against your enemies, to save you... O, strengthen the hands of the IDF soldiers... fight our fight, wage our battle, and spare us in Your kindness... *Ana Hashem hoshiah na, ana Hashem hatzlichah na.* Spare us from danger. Vain is the salvation of man. For God shows might and He will uproot our enemies."

Each stanza brought another soldier to tears. The roll-call response of the tanks and units then followed: "One

Bet, *Amen*"; "Sixteen Dalet, *Amen*"; "Engineering-Gimel, *Amen*"; "One Dalet, *Amen*"...

At 11:40 the first shells fell. Minutes later they were trapped in enemy crossfire. The Israelis were outnumbered, outgunned, and surrounded on both sides of the highway. Missiles crashed in dizzying succession.

Wheee, Boom! Wheee, Boom! BOOM! BOOM! BOOM!!

Earth and asphalt erupted all around; the smell of sulphur filled the air. The tanks broke formation to return the fire. Armored turrets swung back and forth, up and down, as lithe as machine guns in the nimble hands of the gunners. Each volley was returned with double fierceness, but the Syrians overlooking the road bore down. Russian-made shells found their targets. Tanks exploded into raging balls of fire and twisted metal. With each bombardment the remaining tanks became more vulnerable.

The only way to save them was to silence the fire emanating from a building above the highway, an impossible task from the limited scope of a tank. Noam and his crew jumped down from their half-track to try a foot assault.

When they asked Noam why he had enlisted in the army he responded by paraphrasing Rashi's explanation of the verse promising delivery into the Holy Land. "And I will carry you on eagle's wings"... mutav yekanais hachaitz be velo be'achi – *Better the arrow should enter me than my brother...*

Noam advanced off the highway towards the source of the fire. The shells exploding right in front of him were blinding. The earth trembled. He was so exposed, so defenseless. But he was dauntless, determined to advance and protect his comrades. Noam concentrated and fired his machine gun continuously, fearlessly, moving steadily forward from tank to tank.

His unit was made up of *hesder* boys; in each *Merkavah* was a classmate and friend. If he could just get close enough to the building to detonate it, the tanks could fend for themselves.

Some three and a half kilometers to the north, a Soviet Milan missile was being loaded. Somehow the Israeli Airforce missed this launching pad.

Noam's crew followed on his heels. It wasn't too much further to the foot of the building. It was just a matter of time.

A Milan missile has a long white tail of smoke. After it lands, you can study its past.

Noam's crew moved as fast as they could. They had to charge. There was no time to crawl on their bellies.

At noon, right out of the sun, the Milan screamed down. *Better the arrow, yekanais be velo be'achi, should enter me than my brother.*

The Milan sideswiped a tank and sheared off shrapnel in its path. One piece slammed into Noam's chest.

N OAM WAS called up to the war on Friday night. He had returned home from his base that Friday afternoon early enough to take a nap but preferred to help with Shabbos preparations.

Shabbos furlough is nationally observed as a day for sleeping. After the meal he had insisted on staying up for a *shiur* on *parshas hashavua,* heedless to parental pleas that he go to sleep. By the time Noam had finally gone to bed and had managed a few minutes sleep, his unit was called up and he was told to report at once.

It was an emotional scene in the Yehudah home. A call-up, especially on Shabbos, is serious. What can you say? A few brief hugs and kisses and you try not to cry. A lump lodges in your throat and your eyes swim. Peace means sons bury their fathers; war means fathers bury their sons.

Rabbi Yehudah escorted Noam out the door to the courtyard of the Sararya Synagogue. They parted with a *dvar Torah* — it was *parshas Behaaloscha* — *Vayehi Binso'a Ha'aron*.

One week later an *aron* returned and the *levayah* departed from that very spot. Safed stood still on that day. The entire population of the town, joined by hundreds who had travelled for hours to get to that mountain-top city, comprised the funeral procession. It was still the middle of the war, yet 10,000 people attended.

Everyone had a story to tell about Noam:

There was the time he discovered a lonely old man in a home for the aged who couldn't take care of his necessities by himself, until nine-year-old Noam volunteered to help him every day after school.

And the heart attack victim who had no one to visit him. Noam showed up each day with food and a newspaper, feigning interest in the man's stories of World War II...

KAYL *maley rachamim... b'ma'alos kedoshim v'tehorim.* Noam was brought to rest in the Safed cemetery overlooking the *harugei malchus*-victims of the British, the school children killed in Ma'alot and Avivim, and so many other *kedoshim*. Noam had died in the same extended battle.

It was so hard putting him in the earth, he was so young and undeserving of death. Young boys and girls who had never met him, couldn't hold back their tears. They were heirs to Noam's legacy in their schools and youth groups. Veteran army officers felt they had lost a comrade. Noam had treated everyone like family; everyone became a mourner.

David and Shoshana Yehudah and over five hundred other Israeli parents are experts on war. Their lives will never be the same. They join the ranks of thousands of mothers and fathers who have buried their young sons for the sake of peace in the Holy Land.

That Succos, a holiday that the Yehudahs found hard in describing as *chag simchaseinu,* David and Shoshana found the first fruit on Noam's *esrog* tree in their garden. It was *mehudar,* perfectly formed, but small. This year it was just budding. It would be years before the tree would mature and bear a strong, healthy, fragrant crop.

THE EXPLOSION THAT SHOOK UP BAYIT VEGAN

On December 9, 1978 the eighth in a deadly series of terrorist bombs exploded on a number 12 bus as it was letting off passengers in the Bayit Vegan neighborhood of Jerusalem. The blast generated a storm of protest from the residents served by the bus line who felt that the bus company was not providing adequate security.

AT 7:30 in the evening I first found out about an explosion so loud that it had pierced ear drums. All of Hapisga Street shook from the blast. Usually at 7:30 we *daven Maariv* in yeshiva, but that evening a neighbor of mine from Bayit Vegan began to lead the reading of *Tehillim.*

"What happened?" I asked.
"*A bomb just went off on a 12 bus at the Kol Torah Yeshiva stop in Bayit Vegan.*"
"*Hashem yerachem!* That is exactly where I live — my wife should have left work for home on the number 12 bus half an hour ago... Oh, thank God, today is Sunday," I remembered with relief, "the day she visits her grandmother."

Within those few seconds I could almost feel my heart stop beating — that cold clammy feeling which makes you brace for support. My solace was so great that I didn't even think of inquiring about injuries.

After *Maariv* I left for home on the 12 bus. I got off at the Kol Torah stop, kicked away some glass from in front of my building, picked up the mail, and went out to learn. I was amazed at how the evening's tragedy had hardly disturbed me.

After learning for about twenty minutes, a sound truck, the all-too frequent Israeli harbinger of inauspicious news, could be heard in the distance. *"Hakshivu, hakshivu! Toshavei Bayit Vegan, dameinu einenu hefker!..."* "Attention! Attention, residents of Bayit Vegan, our blood is not cheap, a demonstration will be held..." I was bereft of speech. *Dameinu einenu hefker.* Blood was spilled, perhaps a neighbor, a friend, a... and I was barely concerned. As soon as I realized that my wife was not on the bus, I summarily dismissed the incident. Why, I rode the same bus line home! *"Hakshivu, hakshivu toshavei Bayit Vegan!* Residents of Bayit Vegan." We were all in this together.

Later that night I found out that one of the victims had spent Shabbos at our home the day before. Her glasses shattered into her eyes and she was still in shock. It was beginning to hit home. *Where was my sensitivity?*

How could I forget Rav Chaim Shmuelevitz zt'l crying during the first days of the terrorist hijacking to Entebbe: "What would you do if your brother was on that plane?" He was so overcome with emotion that he could not even finish the sentence.

I SPENT that night tossing and turning trying to fall asleep. The message of the sound truck echoed in my ears. Who else heard the message? Were the residents of Mattersdorf, Rechavia, and Boro Park also pained?

In 1882 thousands of Jews gathered in the Frankfurt synagogue for a day of fasting and arousal concerning the sorrowful plight of Russia's pogrom-beleaguered Jews. Rabbi Shamshon Raphael Hirsch preached for three hours to an alms-giving, tearfilled congregation clad in *tallis* and *tefillin*. The gathered included every segment of German

Jewry — even the owners of non-kosher butcher shops and prestigious generals. All remained in the synagogue from dawn to dusk. When Rabbi Simcha Zissel Ziv, the *Alter* of Kelm, learned of this Frankfurt assemblage, he asked, "Why aren't *we* imbued with enough compassion for our brothers to fast and pray on their behalf?" He concluded that those who lack this sensitivity are tantamount to "destroyers of the world."

MONDAY MORNING, Yosel the *melamed* came to *daven* at our sunrise *minyan*. Yosel is one of the *shteiblach* regulars. Even on Friday morning one can't catch Yosel up before 8 a.m. "Only a bomb could get you up with the sun," someone said to him in jest.

"My Leah'la was on that bus," he said with such hurt that we were taken aback. "The slightest noise that we make throws her into hysteria. My house will never be the same..."

Early that evening a local boycott was organized against the 12 bus, aimed at altering its route away from (Arab populated) East Jerusalem. Vans were hired to shuttle residents to and from Mt. Herzl where other bus lines were available. The community was united, but we apparently stood alone. The Ministry of Transportation and the bus company refused to accommodate.

On Tuesday, a demonstration was planned for the following evening. By 6:00 p.m. Wednesday, police units had arrived *en masse* to guarantee that the demonstration remained local, and did not spill over onto Herzl Boulevard. Several army trucks and jeeps were stationed on Mt. Herzl while soldiers rerouted the 12 bus away from Bayit Vegan.

The protestors' angry moods agitated the police. Shouts and clenched fists were aimed at the barricades. Speakers at the protest urged unity; and there was. Such a large collage of knitted *kipot* and black hats was rarely seen in Israel. A momentous event on the one hand, and an incriminating one on the other: Why were we protesting alone? Where was the solidarity of our fellow neighborhoods? — The Frankfurt communities of today? Eight bomb incidents on the 12 bus remained a strictly local problem.

THE 1:00 news that Friday announced the creation of the 39 bus to begin the following month to connect Bayit Vegan and Sanhedria Murchevet, avoiding East Jerusalem. We were somewhat relieved, but the main battle was not yet over. Ludicrous political considerations (one wonders if political considerations would be placed above human ones if a policy-maker's sister would have been on that bus) still forced the 12 bus route to begin in East Jerusalem and terminate in Bayit Vegan (East meets West). Placards were plastered throughout the neighborhood urging a continuance of the boycott.

For the meantime I'll prefer to take the 39 bus. Along side of me will be riding a lesson that the Llelover *Rebbe* zt'l bewailed years ago: The *Rebbe*'s son Moshe was diseased with little hope of recovery. One day the Rebbitzen saw her husband bitterly weeping over Moshe and was also brought to tears. She figured that if her husband was finally crying, Moshe must be close to death.

> *"Moshe'le will be healed with the Almighty's help," the Rebbe comforted his wife, "I am lamenting all the 'Moshe'les' that I see and hear about every day which have never touched my emotions..."*

SUCCESSION OF THE HIGH PRIESTS	SUCCESSION OF THE GENERALS	
CHANIAH I	**ALEXANDER**	
	Ptolemy I	Seleucus I
Elazar		
Menashe		
	Ptolemy II Philadelphius	
Chaniah II	Ptolemy III Eurgetes	Antiochus I
Shimon II	Ptolemy IV	
	Ptolemy V Philopater	Antiochus III
Chaniah III		Seleucus IV
Jason		Antiochus IV Epiphanes
Menelaus (not even a Kohein)		

...INTO THE HANDS OF THE PURE

The victory over the mighty Hellenistic forces climaxing in the purification and rededication of the Temple is mentioned in the Chanukah liturgy. The miracle of the oil which burnt for eight days is commemorated in the kindling of the menora. The Rabbis did not record any other mention of what transpired at the time of the only holiday not mentioned in the Bible. The following is a perspective of the events which preceded those miracles.

THE DREAM of Alexander the Great was to ultimately unite all of his conquered peoples into one great cultural unit. That dream came to an abrupt end with his sudden death at the age of thirty-three. No sooner had he died than the Macedonian empire disintegrated and his generals quarreled among themselves over the control of the lands that he had conquered.

Two of Alexander's successors, generals Ptolemy and Seleucus, are particularly significant in the annals of Jewish history. Ptolemy (whose descendants were called the Ptolemies), gained control of Egypt; and Seleucus (whose descendants were called Seleucids and included Antiochus (III) the Great and Antiochus Epiphanes) inherited most of the land that Alexander had acquired in Asia. Both Ptolemy and Seleucus laid claim to Judea, but Ptolemy succeeded in quickly annexing it.

In the year 3562, Antiochus (III) the Great won a decisive victory over the Egyptian army. It was no secret that the Jews preferred Antiochus' Seleucid-Syrian jurisdiction over the oppressive authority of the Ptolemaic-Egyptians. Until Antiochus III seized power the Jews were at the ruthless mercy of Joseph ben Toviah, the collector of taxes, who was supported by Ptolemy.

Joseph ben Toviah was a maternal nephew of the High Priest Chaniah II, and a priest himself. Far from being a God fearing Jew, he was a regular at Ptolemy Euergetes' table in Egypt[1] and was unscrupulous in his lust for money.

Since the office of the High Priest was hereditary, Joseph ben Toviah had to look for other avenues to achieve power. He was quick to take advantage of his uncle, the High Priest's, weak nature and negligent refusal to pay the customary personal tribute of 20 talents of silver to Ptolemy.

Chaniah II never achieved the legendary piety of his father, Simon the Righteous, and was advanced in age and lacking energy when he acquired the office of High Priest.[2] Chaniah II's failure to pay the tax enraged Ptolemy so much that he sent a representative to Jerusalem who threatened to seize the country, parcel out the land, and settle soldiers throughout Judea.

UNDER THE pretense of saving the country from imminent danger, Joseph usurped his uncle's leadership in supervising the tax collection. As tax collector he was also liable for the country's allegiance to the government, hence he was not merely a financial official but the people's political representative to the king. This delegation of authority was a radical deviation from the existing condition which kept both ecclesiastic and temporal authority exclusively under the High Priest's control.

The role of the High Priest since the time of the Second Temple[3] differed from the office outlined in the Torah.[4] The High Priest's Biblical function was exclusively spiritual and limited, while the temporal leadership of the nation remained in the hands of the king. In the time of Alexander the Great, however, the function of internal government in the civil sphere was under the Sanhedrin's jurisdiction.

The High Priest was assigned the task of tax collection on behalf of foreign rulers as well as supervision over matters of state.[5]

Tax collection has never been popular — especially when collected from a subjugated people. It was regarded as especially hateful when privileged individuals paid the royal treasury a lump sum for the right to collect whatever they could extract from the inhabitants of a district. The system was a cruel one, and King Ptolemy placed a contingent of 2,000 soldiers at the disposal of Joseph and his son to aid in the collection. Joseph mercilessly extracted exorbitant sums from the Jews and did not hesitate to execute recalcitrants and confiscate their property.[6]

Because of the afflictions the Jews suffered at the hands of Joseph ben Toviah and his *mochsim* (tax collectors), the Sanhedrin (and not the High Priest) took the unprecedented action of greeting Antiochus and offering him their allegiance.

In gratitude for the Jews' declared support and the friendly reception Antiochus received when he entered Jerusalem, he issued the following edicts which were proclaimed throughout the kingdom:

> *Compensation was to be made for all damage incurred during the war. The Jews were to be exempt from taxes for three years, to be followed by a reduction of one-third in the amount of taxes due until all reparations were completed. The Sanhedrin, kohanim, Temple scribes and singers were totally exempt from the poll, crown and other taxes. Freedom was to be granted to all those who had been carried away and enslaved.*[7]

Antiochus provided the Jews with domestic and imported timber to rebuild the walls of Jerusalem and the environs of the Temple. He also contributed handsomely to the fund for Temple sacrifices and maintenance. Antiochus prohibited the ritually defiled from entering the Temple precincts, and proscribed the importation of any non-kosher animals or their breeding in Jerusalem. Anyone who violated these edicts was subject to a fine of 3,000 drachmas of silver payable to the High Priest.[8]

Ever since Chaniah II's voluntary, unworthy surrender of power to his nephew Joseph, the Sanhedrin was punctilious in maintaining the Torah's authority over the people amid a growing laxity of Torah standards. The Talmud relates[9] that in those days a Jew who rode a horse on Shabbos was given the death penalty. Under normal circumstances, such a violation does not warrant so serious a punishment, but the nature of the times required no less. Rashi explains that the mitzvos were no longer held in the same esteem and therefore needed strengthening.

THE TRANQUILITY IS SHATTERED

ROME, the reigning power in the world, made it clear to Antiochus not to seek expansion of his kingdom. Antiochus ignored the warning and set out to capture Egypt, a strategically located, well-endowed country. Rome confronted the Seleucid intervention and a war ensued which resulted in a crushing defeat for Antiochus.

Meanwhile, the Jews in Judea continued to enjoy unrestrained freedom to adhere to Torah and mitzvos. The *Book of Maccabees*[10] testifies that, *"the Holy City was governed in a peaceful manner and the laws were preserved due to the piety of the new High Priest, Chaniah*

III (grandson of Chaniah II) and his hatred of evil-doers. Even neighboring kings came to honor and show esteem for the sacred Temple with the finest of gifts."

This tranquility was shattered when Chaniah the High Priest refused to appoint Simon, from the tribe of Benjamin, to an important position. This refusal was seen as a public demonstration against the Hellenizers whom Simon supported. The *Book of Maccabees*[11] reports that, seeking revenge, Simon went

> "to Apollonius of Tarsus, who was at that time governor of Judea and Phonecia. He informed him that aside from what was earmarked for sacrifices, the Temple treasury was teeming with so much gold and silver that it could not even be counted, and recommended that the king hastily expropriate these funds. Apollonius reported this to the king who appointed Heliodorus, his loyal minister, for the mission. When Heliodorus reached Jerusalem, he was graciously received by the High Priest Chaniah III who inquired concerning the purpose of his visit. Heliodorus asked if the information that he had heard about the Temple funds was correct. The High Priest responded that there were deposits entrusted to his care, but they belonged entirely to widows and orphans. Otherwise, everything that the impious Simon had said was an outright lie. It would be unthinkable, he continued, to cause damage to those who relied and were dependent upon this sacred sanctuary, whose dignity and inviolability were universally honored.
>
> "Heliodorus inisted, however, that he could not violate the king's order and was duty-bound to confiscate the money. The city was overcome with grief. On the day that Heliodorus chose to make an inventory of the treasury, the priests prostrated

themselves before the altar and appealed to God. Any man who saw the mien of the High Priest would have been profoundly moved, for his countenance revealed his anguished heart. Fear and trembling seized him; his soul was totally shattered.

"People came rushing out of their houses to join in the communal entreaty, for the Temple was in danger of being defiled. Women dressed in sackcloth crowded the streets; maidens who usually preferred privacy converged on the gates and walls, while some watched from the windows. All stretched forth their hands in supplication to Heaven.

"While the Jews beseeched God to preserve the trusts placed in His sanctuary, Heliodorus and his guards prepared to execute their evil mission. Only a miracle, it seemed, could save them. Suddenly, out of nowhere, the Lord of Hosts caused an apparition in the form of a man to materialize. Heliodorus and all those who accompanied him were struck with panic and faint with fear. A horse with a fearful rider covered with caparisons, came charging at them. At full speed it lunged wildly at Heliodorus with its hoofs. Two robust youths, radiantly beautiful and wearing magnificent apparel also appeared. They stood on both sides of him and flogged him incessantly, inflicting wounds and knocking him unconscious.

"The people witnessed the man who had entered the Temple with a bodyguard and impressive retinue rendered insensible, bereft of all hope of recovery. The entire nation praised God who had miraculously glorified His sacred sanctuary and replaced weeping and sorrow with joy and gladness.

"Heliodorus' friends asked Chaniah III to beseech God to heal their mortally wounded comrade. The High Priest, afraid that the king might think that the Jews had perpetrated this act, offered a sacrifice on

his behalf. As the High Priest was preparing the sacrifice, the two young men arrayed in the same garments reappeared to Heliodorus and said, 'Show your gratitude to the High Priest, for it is because of him that the Lord has spared your life. Proclaim God's sovereign majesty among the nations for you were struck by a heavenly power.' The two men then vanished and Heliodorus offered a sacrifice to God, and made solemn vows to him. Heliodorus blessed Chaniah III and then returned with his soldiers to the king where he testified to the miraculous deeds of the Supreme God.

"The king, however, persisted in his desire to procure the treasury's contents and asked Heliodorus whom he would recommend as an emissary to send to Jerusalem in order to procure the Temple funds. Heliodorus responded, 'If you have an enemy or conspirator against the state, send him there. When he returns, if he shall return at all, he will be soundly flogged, for that sacred place is haunted by a Divine power. God's eyes are on that place and He will surely defend it; whoever enters with evil intentions is as good as dead!'"

SIMON, who had incited Antiochus against the holy Temple when Chaniah III, the High Priest, refused to grant him the position he had coveted, continued to slander Chaniah III and accused him of infidelity to the king and of having personally attacked and injured Heliodorus. Simon was supported by the sons of Joseph, who were the political and moral heirs of their father's venality, and by all of the Hellenizers who enjoyed the protection of Apollonius, the governor of Judea. In order to curtail Simon's slander which could have led to a civil war between the Torah-true Jews and the Hellenists, Chaniah III travelled to Antioch to appeal to King Seleucus (who had succeeded his father King Antiochus III), an ally of the Jews.

Just as he arrived, Seleucus was assassinated and was succeeded by his brother Antiochus IV, who gave himself the surname Epiphanes, "the splendid" but the Jews called him Epimanes, "the madman," and *harasha,* "the wicked." Prior to his acceding to the throne, Antiochus was held in captivity in Rome where he was influenced by the prevalent culture so that he embodied the worst attributes of a Greek and a Roman: lust for exotic pleasures combined with the thirst for war. Antiochus believed that he was a god in flesh and blood destined to realize the practical and total implementation of Hellenization in his kingdom. His religious pretensions had clear political overtones since enforcing the worship of the king served to unite and Hellenize all of his subjects.

He was viewed as a madman not only by the Jews. Antiochus participated in many theatrical performances and enjoyed playing practical jokes on his friends and fellow dignitaries. His eccentricities and leap to power were cunningly exploited by the sons of Joseph and other Hellenizers.

While Chaniah III was still on his mission in Antioch, the Hellenizers illicitly installed Joshua, the brother of Chaniah III, to take over the post of High Priest. Joshua, who changed his name to Jason, was a devoted Hellenist. He usurped his brother by purchasing the office of High Priest from the king for the enormous sum of 440 talents of silver.[12] He promised the king an additional 150 talents if he would be allowed to build a gymnasium and register the people of Jerusalem as Antiocheans. This would virtually annex Jerusalem as a Hellenized city.

KING ANTIOCHUS Epiphanes reversed the benevolent policy of his predecessors towards the Jews. He was delighted by Jason's offer and eagerly accepted it. In order to enlarge his empire and dominate Egypt, it was crucial to Hellenize Judea to create a united Syrian state.

The Sanhedrin, however, prevented Hellenization from progressing in Judea. Most of the Jews were outraged by Antiochus Epiphanes' interference in the succession of the High Priesthood and his treating the sacred office as if it were nothing more than an ordinary governorship. Furthermore, the transfer of the High Priesthood to a brother is not sanctioned by *halacha*.[13]

Jason immediately sought a Greek constitution for Jerusalem, and hoped to develop the city commercially by attaining the right to coin money. Jason and the sons of Joseph realized that Hellenization was the road which would enable Judea to be incorporated into the Seleucid Empire and lead to financial gain. They viewed Chaniah III's firm policy of isolation as stifling to the economy.

Jason was determined not to waste any time in introducing Greek culture. The *Book of Maccabees* records that:

> *"He revoked all of the royal laws and edicts favorable to the Jews and replaced the respectful laws of God with abominable Greek customs. He took delight in establishing a gymnasium right under the citadel, and encouraged the finest of young men to wear the petasus hat. The adoption of Greek customs and zeal for imitating foreign manners due to an ever-growing despicable wickedness of Jason, hardly a High Priest, resulted in the priests' apathy to their duties. Despising the Temple and neglecting the sacrifices, they hastened to participate in the unlawful exercises of the palestra as soon as it came time for discus-throwing. They renounced the values which their fathers esteemed and only considered Greek honors as worthy of attainment."*[14]

Many Jews, including priests, exposed their nude bodies during athletic games. Some priests who participated in the athletics had surgeons draw forward their prepuces so that their circumcision would not be noticeable, and thereby disguise their Jewish origin.

The Jewish masses viewed Jason's activities and their aftermath with revulsion and fear. They saw the sacred office of the High Priest reduced to a degraded political position. The exalted spiritual values and traditions of the Torah were being rapidly abandoned for pagan Hellenism.

THE ESSENCE OF HELLENIZATION IS REVEALED

MANY BELIEVE that Antiochus Epiphanes enacted evil decrees on the Jewish nation on his own initiative, and that the Hellenizers were people lacking the fortitude to stand up to these decrees. This is an error.[15] The Hellenizers were the instigators of the nefarious decrees and forced assimilation. They sought to turn Judea into a Greek province so that the name Israel would no longer be remembered. Antiochus Epiphanes, as wicked as he was, did not aim to destroy the Jewish religion. His overriding interest was power and tribute. Like his predecessors, he realized that the mass of Jews would sacrifice anything to safeguard the sanctity of the Torah's observance.[16]

After having engineered the appointment of Jason as High Priest, the sons of Joseph persistently forged ahead on the road to Hellenization. Having already deviated by installing a High Priest who was not a direct descendant of Chaniah III, the Hellenizers, led by the sons of Joseph continued their renegade policy by appointing a High Priest who was not even of the High Priestly family.

THREE YEARS after Jason's appointment[17] an opportunity to replace him with an even more ardent Hellenizer arose. Jason had dispatched Chaniah, who changed his name to the Greek Menelaus, with the yearly tribute for Antiochus Epiphanes. Menelaus told the king that if appointed High Priest, he would be even more zealous than Jason in carrying out the policy of Hellenization, and offered 300 additional talents of silver above that which Jason had already paid for the office.

Antiochus, who was constantly in need of funds, dismissed Jason from the office of High Priest and appointed Menelaus in his stead. But Jason was unwilling to forfeit his office and a fight broke out between the majority of Jews who sided with Jason, and the sons of Joseph who were supporters of Menelaus.[18] Jason lost the struggle and had to flee for his life. The void that he left was eagerly filled by Menelaus' despotic control of Judea and the High Priesthood.

Menelaus lacked popular support and had to maintain his authority by brute force and terror. He was "like a beast of prey in his wrath,"[19] vehemently despised by the Jews. Menelaus was also in serious trouble because of his inability to raise the sum that he had promised the king. He was duly summoned to Antioch, the Seleucid capital, to account for his breach of the financial agreement. Menelaus took several golden vessels from the Temple along with him to use as payment, or as a bribe if necessary. When he arrived, the king was not in Antioch and the throne was temporarily occupied by Andronicus. Menelaus was able to forge an alliance with Andronicus by bribing him with Temple vessels.

WHEN CHANIAH, the exiled High Priest residing near Antioch, heard about Menelaus' despoiling of the Temple, he was incensed and publicly rebuked him. Menelaus was inflamed by this admonishment. He had always longed to rid himself of his rival, the legitimate High Priest, whose existence posed a threat to his office, and seized upon this opportunity to persuade Andronicus to execute Chaniah III. Andronicus furtively went to Chaniah's asylum and

> "giving him his right hand swore his security. In spite of his lurking suspicion, Chaniah was persuaded to leave the sanctuary. As soon as he left, Andronicus put him ruthlessly to death."[20]

The Jews were not the only ones appalled by this cold-blooded murder. The *Book of Maccabees* records that:

> "When the king returned from the country of Cilia, the Jews and the Greeks, who were also revulted by the villainous deed, obtained an audience with Antiochus concerning the unjust murder of Chaniah. The king was sincerely grieved and was even moved to pity and tears because he recognized the well-ordered life of the victim. Enraged with passion, Antiochus tore off the purple robe and tunic from Andronicus, paraded him in dishonor through the city to the very spot where he had committed the outrage against Chaniah, and killed the vile murderer."[21]

Menelaus managed to escape Antiochus' wrath, but his position in Jerusalem was in jeopardy. Before leaving Jerusalem for Antioch, he had appointed his brother, Lysimachus, to act as High Priest in his absence and to raise the necessary funds for the king in any expedient manner. Lysimachus duly proceeded to execute the despoliation of the Temple treasury, a blatantly sacrilegious act which aroused the indignation and ire of the Jerusalem population. The Temple treasury had a special sanctity and was donated by all of Israel. It was unthinkable to tolerate a small group of infidels, vociferously non-Jewish in their lifestyle and activities, disposing of it as if it were their own private funds. The despicable character of Hellenization was now obvious to everyone and the people were ripe for rebellion.

Crowds rioted in Jerusalem. Lysimachus armed 3,000 men and pitched battles were fought in the streets. The people "picked up stones and sticks while others clutched handfuls of cinders that were lying about and hurled them at Lysimachus' men, causing utter confusion."[22] The masses were victorious and even succeeded in killing Lysimachus in this first act of rebellion.

THE SAGES of Jerusalem were scandalized by the crimes Menelaus and his brother had perpetrated. They sent a delegation of three Sanhedrin members to Antiochus to level charges against Menelaus for stealing the golden Temple vessels. Menelaus bribed one of the king's officers with one of those very stolen vessels, and the officer in turn persuaded the sovereign that Menelaus was innocent of all evil. In a cruelly ironic turn of events, the three members of the Sanhedrin were sentenced to death instead of Menelaus, who returned victorious to Jerusalem as the High Priest, invested with more authority by the king than he had possessed before. Upon his return to Jerusalem he intensified the policy of Hellenization[23] and temporarily succeeded in suppressing the proliferating seeds of revolt.

War erupted around the year 3590 between Antiochus Epiphanes and Egypt. Antiochus' stunning victory marked the first time since the era of Alexander the Great that Egypt was successfully invaded from Judea. Returning in triumph from Egypt, Antiochus invaded Jerusalem with the aim to replenish his revenues which were depleted by the Egyptian campaign. He entered the Temple and confiscated *"the golden altar, the menora and all its equipment, the table of the show bread, the cups, the bowls and the golden censers, the crowns, and the golden adornment on the front of the Sanctuary,"*[24] — without the slightest regard for the Temple's sanctity or the people's feelings. The mournful protests of the people were met with bloody massacres.

ANTIOCHUS' REVENGE

IT WAS about this time[25] that Antiochus returned to Egypt and an ominous apparition appeared in the Jerusalem skies. The Book of Maccabees describes that

> "fully armed horsemen, clad in robes embroidered in pure gold, arrayed attack and counterattack launched from one side, then from the other with shaking of shields and massing of spear shafts and unleashing of swords, casting of darts, flashing of gold trappings and breastplates of every kind"[26]

appeared for about forty days in the sky. This awesome apparition was interpreted as an auspicious omen by the Jews, who were aware that Antiochus' military advances were being checked by Rome. A false rumor began to circulate that Antiochus had died, and repercussions were felt all over the kingdom. Jason, who had been deposed by Menelaus, now returned to Jerusalem with an army of about 1,000 men. Menelaus fled to the city's citadel while Jason wreaked havoc upon the citizens.

When news of these events reached Antiochus he assembled his army at once. Antiochus viewed the uprising in Jerusalem not merely as a fratricidal war but as an uprising against himself and he was determined to quash it forever. Furthermore, having recently lost Egypt to Rome he wanted to keep Judea securely in rein and have Judea serve as a buffer in the face of an Egyptian attack. "Gripped by wild animal fury," he launched a powerful attack against the defenseless Jews slaying some 40,000 and an equal number were sold into slavery.[27]

THE HEROIC MARTYRDOM

Now THAT Antiochus' political measures had been carried out, he began to institute systematic religious persecution, referred to as the *gezeiros hashmad*. The Temple was rededicated to Zeus-Olympus, and the observance of Sabbath, circumcision and *Rosh Chodesh* was prohibited under penalty of death.[28] Temple worship was replaced with forbidden sacrifices, profane acts and orgies. The Jews were forced to celebrate the king's birthday every month and to participate in the festal procession in honor of Dionysus.[29] On the 25th of Kislev a heathen altar, "The Abomination of Desolation," was erected on the site of the Temple altar and a swine was sacrificed on it.[30] Menelaus was no longer the High Priest of the God of Israel, but a priest subordinate to Antiochus Epiphanes.

Most Jews viewed these events with hearts heavy with dread, but what could they do against the rich and mighty? The Sages ruled that since the Greeks were intent upon exterminating Judaism, the principle of *Yeyhareig Ve'al Ya'avor* applied: one must lay down his life rather than transgress any mitzva thereby sanctifying God's name.[31] Courageous Jews, known as the *Chassidim*,[32] were meticulous in adhering to all the mitzvos, even in the face of torture and death. Their resolution was a *kiddush Hashem* (sanctification of God's name) that could not be easily dismissed, even by their Greek oppressors.

The *Book of Maccabees*[33] records how a thousand Jews fled the city to a cave in order to observe the (outlawed) Shabbos. When Antiochus' agents discovered their whereabouts, they threatened to burn them alive in the cave unless they would come out and profane the

Shabbos. The Jews, offering no resistance, refused to violate the holy Shabbos. Soldiers amassed timber at the entrance of the cave and set it ablaze burning all of the men, women and children alive.

These thousand and countless other martyrs endured excruciating tortures and sacrificed their lives to sanctify the Almighty's name. The accounts of Elazar and of Chanah and her seven sons highlight the torment and affliction the Jews suffered.

ELAZAR, a 90-year-old, distinguished Jew, was coerced to eat swine publicly. His jaw was pried open and swine was brutally forced down his throat.[34] The unyielding Elazar disgorged the food with revulsion. Either out of admiration or pity, the Hellenists who had committed this atrocity were surprisingly touched by the courage of the sage. They pleaded with him to eat perfectly kosher meat to make it appear as if he were complying with the royal command, and thereby save his life. Elazar was unwilling to yield lest he mislead his Jewish brethren, and was flogged to death. In his final agony, he uttered an immortal testimony: "The Lord in His sacred knowledge is aware that although I could have escaped this terrible suffering, I endure it gladly because of my reverence for the Eternal."[35]

CHANA*[36] and her seven sons were arrested and compelled by the king to prostrate themselves before an idol.** The eldest son was the first one brought before Antiochus and ordered to bow before the image.

---

* In the *Gemorah Gittin* she is called "a woman with seven sons." In *Eicha Rabbati* she is called Miriam bas Nachtum. In Josephus Book 19 she is referred to as Chana.

** In the *Book of Maccabees*, to eat swine's meat.

"God forbid shall I bow down to an idol," he said. *"For it says in the Torah, 'I am the Lord your God.' " (Shmos 20:2)* In his rage the king commanded that pans and caldrons be heated red hot. He ordered the boy's tongue cut out, his head scalped, and his extremities chopped off, while his brothers and mother were forced to look on. When he had been reduced to a completely useless, barely breathing hulk he was brought to the fire and fried in the pan. As the heinous vapor grew dense the children and their mother encouraged each other to die nobly saying, *"The Lord God is watching, and is sure to have compassion on us. Moshe has thus declared in his song 'And He will have compassion upon His servants.' " (Devarim 32:36)*

The second son was brought before the king who commanded him to prostrate himself. *"God forbid,"* he replied. *"My brother did not bow before the idol and neither shall I. It is written in the Torah 'You shall have no other gods before me.' " (Shmos 20:3)* Upon hearing this the king ordered him to be slain.

The Greeks then brought the third son before the king who ordered him to prostrate before the image. *"I will not bow down for it is written in the Torah, 'You shall not bow down to any other god.' " (Shmos 34:14)* And the king ordered that he be put to death.

They brought forth the next son who quoted *"He that sacrifices unto the gods, save unto the Lord, shall be destroyed," (Shmos 22:19)* and was led away to his death.

When the fifth son was commanded to prostrate to the image he quoted: *"Hear O Israel, the Lord our God, the Lord is One" (Devarim 6:4)* and was immediately ordered to be slain.

The sixth son was then brought to the king who commanded him to prostrate himself before the image. The boy answered that it is written in the Torah, *"The Lord your*

God is in your midst, a God great and awful," (Devarim 7:21) and was taken to his death.

THE SEVENTH SON, the youngest of them all, was then brought before the king. Desperate to have his way, the following discussion between the king and the boy ensued:

"My son, prostrate yourself before the image."
"God forbid! It is written in our Torah 'Know this day and lay it in your heart that the Lord He is God in heaven above and upon the earth beneath; there is none else.' (Devarim 4:39) We have sworn that we will not exchange Him for any other god as it says, 'You have proclaimed the Lord this day to be your God.' (Devarim 26:17) And as we swore to Him, He has sworn to us not to exchange us for another people as it says, 'The Lord proclaimed you today to be His own treasure.' " (Devarim 26:18)

"Your brothers had their fill of years and experienced life and happiness, but you are young and have not tasted life or happiness. Serve the idol and I will bestow favors and treasures upon you."

"It is written in our Torah 'The Lord shall reign forever and ever.' (Shmos 15:18) The Lord is King forever; the nations are perished out of His land. (Tehillim 10:16) You, Antiochus, are of no account and neither are the rest of His enemies. A human being lives today and is gone tomorrow, but the Holy One blessed be He, lives and endures forever and ever!"

"Your brothers are slain before you," implored the king. *"Behold, I will throw my ring down to the ground in front of the image; bend down and pick it up so that all will think that you have obeyed my command."*

"Chaval alecha Kaisar, chaval alecha Kaisar. It is

a pity upon you O King! If you are afraid of human beings who are the same as yourself, shall I not fear the Supreme King of Kings, the Holy One blessed be He, the God of the Universe! The true God is not like the false Greek gods which have no mouth, eyes, ears, nose, hands, feet, throat, etc..."

"If your God has all of these attributes, why doesn't He deliver you out of my hand like He rescued Channaniah, Mishael and Azariah from the hands of Nevuchadnezzar?"

"Channaniah, Mishael and Azariah were worthy men, and King Nevuchadnezzar was deserving that a miracle be performed through him. You, however, are hardly deserving; and as for ourselves, we forfeit our lives to heaven. If you do not slay us, the Omnipresent has various means. There are many bears, wolves, serpents, leopards and scorpions to kill us, but in the end the Holy One, blessed be He, will avenge our blood upon you.

HUMILIATED by this young boy, the king ordered him to be put to death. The child's mother beseeched the king: *"By your life O king, give me my son that I may kiss and embrace him."* She took the baby, uncovered her breast and began to nurse him.

"By your life O king," she exclaimed, *"put me to death before you slay him."*

"I cannot grant you your request," the king responded, *"for it is written in your Torah 'Whether it be cow or sheep you may not kill it and its young both in one day.'"* (Vayikra 22:28)

"You incredible fool," she retorted. *"Have you already fulfilled all the other commandments in the Torah that you lack just this one?!"* He immediately ordered the babe to be

slain. She threw herself upon her child and wept:

> "My son, go tell Avraham Avinu that thus said your mother: Do not pride yourself in your righteousness saying that 'I built an altar and offered up my son Yitzchak.' Behold our mother built seven altars and offered seven sons in one day. Yours was only a trial of faith, but mine was the actual deed!"

While tearfully embracing and kissing him the king issued the command and they killed the child in her arms. A heavenly voice rang out and proclaimed "*Aim habanim smaicha*" — mother of the children who rejoices (*Tehillim* 113:9) and the Holy Spirit cried out, "*For these do I weep.*" (*Eichah* 1:16)[37]

THE GREEKS also decreed that any Jew who had a lock on his door would be put to death.[38] The Jews could no longer eat or drink in peace nor have marital relations for fear of robbers and Greek intruders.

> *A man whose wife went to the mikvah would be executed. Whoever desired the woman was free to take her for a wife and her children for slaves. With no alternative, the Jews curtailed their marital relations*[39] *until a mikvah miraculously appeared in their homes.*[40]

The Greeks then proclaimed that before marriage all Jewish women must first have relations with the ruler.[41] And when the daughter of Mattisyahu ben Yochanan the High Priest was to be wed, her father and five brothers would not allow her to be defiled. And the battle cry rang out: "*Mi Lashem Ailai*" — "Whoever follows *Hashem*, join me!"[42]

Notes

1. Josephus, *Antiquities*, Book XII, 4:3.
2. Gutkowski, J., *The Era of the Second Temple (Tkufas Bayis Sheini)*, p. 97.
3. Breuer, *Divrei Hayamim LeYisrael U'le'umos HaOlam*, p. 210.
4. *Vayikra*, 21:10.
5. HaLevy, *Doros Harishonim, Tkufah Haemtza'is*, ch. 10.
6. Josephus, *Antiquities*, Book XII, 4:5.
7. *Ibid.*, 3:3.
8. *Ibid.*
9. *Sanhedrin*, 46.
10. The Second Book of Maccabees, ch. 3.
11. *Ibid.*
12. *Ibid.*, 4:8,9.
13. Rambam, *Peirush HaMishnah* on *Menachos*, 109.
14. *Op. cit.*, 2:4.
15. HaLevy, *loc. cit.*, ch. 6: *Tzedukim U'baitusim*.
16. *Op. cit.*, ch. 10.
17. The Second Book of Maccabees, ch. 4.
18. Josephus, *Antiquities*, Book XII, 5:1.
19. *Op. cit.*, 4:25.
20. *Ibid.*, 4:34.
21. *Ibid.*, 4:34-8.
22. *Ibid.*, 4:41.
23. *Ibid.*, 4:50.
24. The First Book of Maccabees, 1:22-24.
25. *Op. cit.*, 5:2-3.
26. *Ibid.*
27. *Ibid.*, 5:11.
28. The Scroll of the Hasmoneans, 9.
29. *Ibid.*, ch. 6.
30. *Op. cit.*, 1:53.
31. Rabinowitz, *Hadrachah BeLimud Toldos Yisrael*, p. 92.
32. Gutkowski, *Tkufas Bayis Sheini*, p. 141.
33. The First Book of Maccabees, ch. 2.
34. The Second Book of Maccabees, ch. 6.

35. *Ibid.*
36. *Eichah Rabbah,* 1:50.
37. *Ibid.*
38. Minchen, *Midrash Ma'aseh Chanukah,* as quoted in *Toldos Am Olam,* R. Sh. Rottenberg.
39. *Ibid.*
40. *Baal Haturim* on *Breishis,* 26:22.
41. *Kesubos,* 3.
42. Rottenberg, Sh., *Toldos Am Olam,* Vol. 2, Sect. 4, ch. 1.

Glossary

The following glossary provides a partial explanation of some of the Hebrew and Yiddish words and terms used in this book. Both the spelling and explanations reflect the way the specific word is used in *Once Upon a Soul*. Often, there are alternate spellings and meanings for the words. Hebrew and Yiddish words and terms which are immediately followed by a translation in the text are not included in this glossary.

ACHRONIM — talmudic scholars of the last five hundred years

AGUNAH — lit. a "chained woman;" refers to a woman whose marriage has been terminated *de facto* but not *de jure*, and who is therefore incapable of remarrying because she is still technically married to her absent husband

AIFO — where

ALEINU LESHABEI'ACH — our duty to praise — prayer said at the conclusion of all services, and at the side of the death bed

ALEPH-BAIS — the Hebrew alphabet

ALIYAH — going up; term used in connection with 1. being called up to the reading of the Torah; 2. immigration to Israel

ALIYAS REGEL — holiday pilgrimage to Jerusalem

ALTER — (Yid.) aged one; a title of respect

AMMORAH — a scholar of the talmudic period

ANA HASHEM HOSHIAH NA — please, God, save us

ANA HASHEM HATZLICHA NA — please, God, prosper us

ANIYIM — poor people

APIKORUS — heretic

APIKORUS KOTTON — small heretic

ARON — coffin

ARON KODESH — lit. holy ark; ark containing the Torah scrolls

ASKINU SEUDASA — lit. prepare the feast; a kabbalistic hymn in Aramaic sung at the Sabbath meal

AVRAHAM AVINU — Abraham our father

BAAL HABATTIM — lay individuals

BAAL KOREH — reader of the Torah

BAAL TEFILLA — leader of prayer

BAAL TESHUVA (f. BAALAS TESHUVA) — penitent who has returned to religious observance

BAMIDBAR — Book of Numbers

BARUCH ATTA HASHEM — blessed are You God

BECHOR — first-born male

BEIS DIN (TZEDEK) — court of Jewish law

BEIS MIDRASH — house of study used for both Torah study and prayer

BEKASHE — caftan

BEN SHMONIM — man in his eighties

BENTCHER — blessing booklet containing Grace after Meals

BIRKAS HACHAMAH — blessing over the sun recited every twenty-eight years

BIRKAS KOHANIM — blessing of the nation by descendants of Aaron's priestly family

BOCHUR (BOCHURIM) — unmarried yeshiva student

BRACHA — blessing

BRACHA, HATZLACHA, VECHOL TUV — blessing, success and all the best

BRIS — The Jewish rite of circumcision

CHACHAM — wise man; "rabbi" in Sephardic circles

CHEDER (CHADORIM) — lit. room; yeshiva elementary school

CHABURA (CHABUROS) — gathering where talmudic insights are discussed

CHAG — holiday

CHAG SIMCHASEINU — lit. holiday of our rejoicing; Succos

CHAS VESHALOM — God forbid

CHASSIDISHE — chassidic

CHATZOS — midnight

CHAVRUSA — study partner

CHAZAL — 1. acronym of our sages of blessed memory; 2. a statement by the sages

CHAZON ISH — Rabbi Avraham Yeshayahu Karelitz zt'l (1878-1953); from the time that he settled in Bnei Brak, Israel, he became a leading figure in Jewish law and life

CHAZORES HASHATZ — cantor's repetition of the *Shemona Esrei*

CHAZZAN — cantor; the leader of public worship

CHAZZANUS — cantillation

CHESSED — deeds of lovingkindness

CHIDDUSH — novellae; new insights in Torah interpretation; e.g. *Chiddushei HaRashba* — novellae of the Rashba

CHINUCH ATZMAI — network of Torah schools in Israel enjoying the endorsement of the leading rabbis

CHOLEH — a sick person

CHOMETZ — leaven which results when either wheat, barley, spelt, rye, or oats remain in contact with water for a period of time before baking; the Torah forbids eating or deriving any benefit from *chometz* on Passover

CHOSHEN MISHPAT — one of the four sections of *The Code of Jewish Law* which deals with torts

CHASSAN — groom

CHUMASH — set of the five books of the Torah; any of the five books

DAVEN — (Yid.) pray

DEVORIM — Book of Deuteronomy

DROSHA — learned discourse

DVAR TORAH — a Torah thought

ELIYAHU HANAVI — Elijah the Prophet

ELUL — last month of the Hebrew calendar preceding Rosh Hashanah

EREV — eve

FRUM — (Yid.) religious

GABBAI (GABBOIM) TZEDDAKA — warden who collects and dispenses charity

GADOL — lit. great one; refers to a giant in Torah scholarship

GALUS — exile; Diaspora

GA'ON — lit. brilliant one; title of honor for a distinguished sage

GEDOLEI HADOR — greatest Torah scholars of the generation

GEMORAH — 1. commentary on the Mishna (together they comprise the Talmud); 2. a volume of the Talmud

GET — (gittin) divorce document

GOLDENNA MEDINA — (Yid.) country of gold

GORAL HAGRA — lit. lottery of the Vilna Ga'on; method of determining action in accord with the implications of a biblical verse which lands in a lottery

GOY (GOYIM) — lit. nation, Gentile

HAKOFOS — seven joyous revolutions made around the Torah scrolls on the holiday of Simchas Torah

HALACHA — Jewish law

HALACHA LEMA'ASEH — practical application of Jewish law

HAMOTZI — the blessing made over bread

HAR HABAYIS — the Temple Mount

HAR HAMENUCHOS — mountain at the entrance to Jerusalem; site of a large cemetery

HARUGEI MALCHUS — lit. murdered victims of the regime; martyrs

HASHEM — lit. The Name; respectful reference to God

HASHEM HU HAELOKIM — God He is the Lord

HASHEM YERACHEM — may God have compassion

HASHGACHA PRATIS — Divine Providence

HAVARA — pronunciation

HESDER — combined yeshiva study and military service

HOSHANAH RABBA — the seventh day of Succos

KABBALOS HATORAH — acceptance of the Torah

KALLAH — bride

KASHAS — questions

KASHRUS — kosherness, Torah dietary regulations

KAYL MALEY RACHAMIM ...B'MAALOS KEDOSHIM VETEHORIM — lit. God full of compassion... may the soul rest among the holy and pure; prayer for the deceased

KEHILLA — organized community; congregation

KEIN YIRBU — biblical blessing to increase that which is good e.g. children

KEVER ROCHEL — tomb of Rachel

KIDDUSH — sanctification; prayer recited over wine to usher in the Sabbath and festivals

KIDDUSH HASHEM — sanctification of God's name; martyrdom

KIPA (KIPOS) — skullcap; head covering worn by religious Jews

KLAL YISRAEL — community of Israel; all of Jewry

KOHEIN (KOHANIM) — a male descendant from the priestly family of Aaron

KOLLEL — post-graduate yeshiva whose student body is usually comprised of young married students who receive stipends.

KORIM — the section of the *Aleinu Leshabei'ach* prayer where, on Rosh Hashana and Yom Kippur, one goes down on his knees

KOSEL (HAMA'ARAVI) — lit. Western Wall; last remaining wall of the Temple courtyard and eminent holy site

LAG B'OMER — the thirty-third day of the counting of the *Omer* (days between the second day of Passover and Shavuos), and also the anniversary of the death of Rabbi Shimon bar Yochai; on this day Jews may interrupt the mourning observed during the *Omer*

LANDSMAN — (Yid.) fellow townsman

LECHA DODI — a song in the Friday night service, composed by Solomon Alkabetz HaLevi; it refers to the Sabbath as the bride of the Jewish people

MAARIV — evening prayer

MACHLOKES — dispute; polemic

MAZAL — luck; good fortune

ME'ATTA VE'AD OLAM — from now and forever more

MEDINA — state

MEHUDAR — perfectly formed

MELAMED — teacher

MERKAVAH — Israeli-produced tank

MESECHTA — talmudic volume

MESHUMED — convert from Judaism

MESILAS YESHARIM — lit. path of the straight; classic in ethics written by Rabbi Moshe Chaim Luzzatto

MIDDOS — character traits

MIKVAH — a ritual bath used for the purpose of ritual purification

MINYAN (MINYANIM) — quorum of ten adult Jewish males; the basic unit of community for certain religious purposes, including prayer

MISHMAR — lit. watch; an all night Torah study session

MISHNA — the earliest codification of Jewish oral law by Rabbi Yehudah Hanassi

MISNAGID (MISNAGDIM) — opposer of chassidic movement

MODEH ANI — lit. I render thanks; prayer said upon rising in the morning

MOHEL — one who performs the religious ceremony of circumcision

MOSHIACH — the Messiah

MOTZEI — the evening after

MUSSAR — 1. school of thought emphasizing ethical perfection; 2. moral teachings; 3. ethical lecture

NA'ASEH VENISHMA — we will do and then comprehend; Israelite response to God's offer of the Torah

NACHAS — 1. joy; 2. positive fulfillment

NISHT GEFAIRLACH — (Yid.) not so bad

PAROCHES — curtain of the ark containing the Torah scrolls

PARSHAS HASHAVUA — the weekly Torah portion

PAYOS — sidelocks

PESACH — Passover

PESUKEI DEZIMRAH — beginning section of morning prayer

PIDYON PETER CHAMOR — redemption of first-born male ass

POSKIM — halachic authorities

REBBE (REBBEIM) — 1. rabbi, usually a Talmud teacher; 2. instructor; 3. chassidic leader

REPHAENU — lit. heal us, prayer in *Shemona Esrei* beseeching Divine healing

RESHUS LECHASSAN TORAH — invitation to the most prestigious *aliyah* given to the greatest Torah scholar present on *Simchas Torah*

RISHON (RISHONIM) — lit. first one; European scholars of the eleventh through the fifteenth century

ROSH CHODESH — beginning of the month

ROSH YESHIVA (ROSHEI YESHIVA) — yeshiva dean

SEDER — 1. the festive celebration on the first and (in the Diaspora) second nights of Passover where the story of the Exodus from Egypt is recited; 2. study session in a yeshiva

SEFER (SEFARIM) — book of religious content

SEFER TEHILLIM — book of Psalms

SEFER TORAH — Torah scroll

SMICHA — rabbinic ordination

SEUDA SHLISHIS — the third Sabbath meal, usually begun just before sunset lasting past nightfall

SEUDAS MITZVA — 1. meal at a religious ceremony; 2. meal which is the fulfillment of a precept

SEUH SHEARIM ROSHEICHEM — lit. lift your heads O gates, a verse in Psalm 24

SHACH — abbreviation for Sifsei Cohen; Rabbi Shabsi Cohen, who wrote a commentary on *Shulchan Aruch*

SHACHARIS — the morning prayers; service

SHAMASH — synagogue caretaker; rabbi's assistant

SHECHALAK — lit. who has bestowed; blessing recited when seeing a monarch

SHECHINA — the Divine Presence

SHEHECHIYANU — lit. who has granted us life; blessing recited on special occasions

SHEMA YISRAEL — prayer recited daily proclaiming the oneness of God and affirming faith in Him and His Torah

SHEMONA ESREI — 1. lit. eighteen; the central prayer in Jewish liturgy which is recited three times daily

SHEVA BRACHOS — 1. the seven benedictions recited at a wedding and in the presence of the newlyweds during the first week of their marriage; 2. the seven days after a wedding

SHIR HAMA'ALOS — lit. song of degrees; 1. chapter from Psalms said just before grace after meals; 2. introductory words to several chapters in Psalms

SHIUR (SHIURIM) — Torah lecture

SHIVA — lit. seven, the seven-day period of mourning following death

SHIVA ASSAR BETAMMUZ — the seventeenth day of the month of Tammuz; a fast day which commemorates five tragedies, including the breaking of the wall around Jerusalem

SHKIA — sunset

SHKOACH — abbreviation of *yasher koach*

SHMOS — Book of Exodus

SHOMER — guardian

SHTEIBEL (SHTEIBLACH) — (Yid.) small, informal intimate room for prayer or study

SHTENDER — lectern, used in place of desks in many yeshivos

SHTETEL — (Yid.) village

SHTREIMAL (SHTREIMLACH) — (Yid.) decorative fur hat

worn by male chassidim on Sabbath and festivals

SHUL — (Yid.) synagogue

SHULCHAN ARUCH — code of Jewish law compiled by Rabbi Yosef Karo

SIDDUR — prayer book

SIYUM — completion ceremony

SOFREIHEM — their sages

SUCCAH — temporary dwelling which is a central requirement of the holiday of Succos

SUCCOS — Autumn holiday held five days after Yom Kippur during which time one dwells in a succah

SUGYA — talmudic topic

TALLIS — four-cornered prayer shawl with fringes at each corner worn by men during morning prayers

TALMID CHACHAM (TALMIDEI CHACHAMIM) — Torah scholar

TANACH — Scriptures (Torah, Prophets, Writings)

TANYA — book by Rabbi Shneur Zalman of Liadi in which the principles of Lubavitch are expounded; the name is derived from the initial word of the work

TAZ — acronym for Turei Zahav; commentator on the code of Jewish law

TEFILLA — prayer

TEFILLIN — black leather boxes containing verses from the Bible bound to the arm and head of a man during morning prayer

TEHILLIM — Psalms

TESHUVA — repentance

TICHEL(S) — (Yid.) woman's scarf used to cover her hair

TIKUN CHATZOS — midnight prayers mourning the destruction of the Temple and imploring its restoration

TREIF — lit. torn; non-kosher; unacceptable

TZADDIK (TZADDIKIM) — righteous man

TZEDDAKA — charity

TZ'ENAH UR'ENAH — book written in Yiddish for women relating the stories of the Torah

TZIDKUS — righteousness

VAAD (VAADIM) — informal groups usually to discuss mussar topics

VAAD HAYESHIVOS — committee of the yeshivos; intermediary between the Israeli army and yeshiva students receiving a draft deferral

VAYEHI BINSO'A HA'ARON — "and it was whenever the ark journeyed," words in Behaaloscha; Numbers 10:35, discussing the travelling of the ark, *aron*

VAYIKRA — Book of Leviticus

YASHER KOACH (SHKOACH) — well done

YERUSHALAYIM SHEL MA'ALAH — lit. Jerusalem of above

YIDDEN GIBB TZEDDAKA — (Yid.) Jews give charity

YIRAH — lit. fear; fear of heaven

YOM KIPPUR KOTTON — set of prayers and supplications said by some on *Rosh Chodesh* eve resembling part of the Yom Kippur liturgy

YOM TOV — holiday

YOMIM NORAIM — days of awe; ten days of penitence beginning on Rosh Hashanah through Yom Kippur

YOREH DE'AH — one of the four sections of the code of Jewish law

YUNGERMAN — (Yid.) young married man

ZECHUS — merit

ZT'L — abbreviation for *tzaddik* of blessed memory

Q. What brand new publication has more subscriptions than Jewish periodicals that have been around for a quarter of a century or more?

A. Hanoch Teller's **StoryLines**, a tri-annual "story-letter" for the whole family.

Here's Why:

Each inspiring tale in **StoryLines** is an original gem written by the king of storytellers, **Hanoch Teller**, whose stories have delighted and uplifted Jewish audiences for over a decade.

Attractively designed and produced on high-quality paper, each issue has a timely story about the holiday it heralds. Acclaimed by parents and educators alike, each issue of **StoryLines** includes: a feature-length story annotated with a vocabulary-expanding glossary, a biography of a *tzaddik* or *tzaddekes* for teenagers, an easy-to-read tale for beginners, a cartoon episode of "Velvel the Wagon Driver," a teachers' guide for effective use of all the material, and much more.

StoryLines subscribers can take advantage of spectacular savings on books and cassettes not available elsewhere.*

Join the **StoryLines** sensation and receive a delightful "story-letter" three times a year: Rosh Hashana, Chanuka, and Purim. It's entertaining, intriguing, informative, and educational. You'll cherish every word. Subscribe today — don't be left out!

* **StoryLines** *is only available through subscription*

HANOCH TELLER's
StoryLines
Stories for the whole family
37 West 37th St. 4th Fl. New York, NY 10018

127 Woodstock Ave. London NW11 9RL   3 Prince Charles Dr. Toronto M6A2H1   Arzei Habirah 46/7 Jerusalem 97781